History on Our Plate

History on Our Plate

Recipes from America's Dutch
Past for Today's Cook

Peter G. Rose

Syracuse University Press

Much of this material previously appeared in *Matters of Taste: Food and Drink in Seventeenth-Century Dutch Art and Life*, Donna R. Barnes and Peter G. Rose, eds. (Albany Institute of History & Art/Syracuse University Press, 2002).

For a listing of books published and distributed by Syracuse University Press, visit https://press.syr.edu.

ISBN: 978-0-8156-1118-9 (paperback)

Library of Congress Cataloging-in-Publication Data
Names: Rose, Peter G., author. | Barnes, Donna R. Matters of taste.
Title: History on our plate : recipes from America's Dutch past for today's cook / Peter G. Rose.
Description: First edition. | Syracuse : Syracuse University Press, 2019. | Includes bibliographical references and index. | Summary: "This volume— an updated, expanded edition of the cookbook companion to "Matters of Taste: Food and Drink in Seventeenth-Century Dutch Art and Life"— brings a sampling of historical Dutch cooking to the modern kitchen, offering delicious recipes for cookies and custards as well as savory dishes and salads. With an added section on advice for children's participation, the author aims to make the book accessible and enjoyable for everyone, and to prove that historical cooking—whether done over an open fire or on a stove top—need not be a thing of the past"—Provided by publisher.
Identifiers: LCCN 2019036587 | ISBN 9780815611189 (paperback)
Subjects: LCSH: Cooking, Dutch. | Cooking, American—History—17th century. | LCGFT: Cookbooks.
Classification: LCC TX723.5.N4 R67 2019 | DDC 641.59492—dc23
LC record available at https://lccn.loc.gov/2019036587

TO DON & PETER PAMELA

For the past, the present, and the future

Contents

Acknowledgments

I WOULD LIKE TO THANK Consul General of the Kingdom of the Netherlands to New York, Dolph Hogewoning, for his kind words about my work. My sincerest thanks to Charles T. Gehring, PhD, director of The New Netherland Research Center at the New York State Library in Albany, NY. He has always been immensely helpful and ready to answer questions. On top of that he is a great cook with a lively interest in historical recipes and culinary information of the New Netherland period.

My sincerest thanks also to Professor Emerita Donna R. Barnes, EdD, now deceased, for several decades of collaboration. She was my co-curator on the exhibit "Matters of Taste" at the Albany Institute of History & Art in 2002 and co-author on several books, including the exhibit's catalog. She is deeply missed by her relatives and many friends.

I am most fortunate to be able to call culinary historian Stephen Schmidt my friend, and I am deeply grateful to him for all his help with this recipe book and other projects over the past 20 years or more.

Dutch culinary historian Joop Witteveen and Dutch culinary journalist Johannes van Dam, both now deceased, have always been helpful and interested in my work, for which I am very thankful.

Over the last 10 years, Michael Schechter, president of Computer Experts Group, Ltd. in Katonah, NY, has helped me with my computer problems. Without his kind, quick, and patient assistance my work would not be possible.

Physical therapist Jeanne Morgante, PT, DPT, MTC, has literally "straightened me out" and made it possible for me to spend the necessary long hours at the computer to get this and other jobs done. I dedicate the pretzel recipe to her.

In addition, I would like to express my gratitude to the following: Delphina Brownlee Bashkow, Peter de Jong, Tessa Dikker, Joe DiMauro, Mary Selden Evans, Jonathan Z. Friedman, Dennis Maika, PhD, senior historian and education director of the New Netherland Institute, Susan Simon, Esq., for expert legal advice, well-known art collector George Way, now deceased, Dutch culinary historian Marleen van der Molen Willebrands, and Professor Emerita Dr. Johanna Maria van Winter, and to Alice Randel Pfeiffer, director of Syracuse University Press, and my editors, Kelly L. Balenske, Suzanne E. Guiod, Marcia Hough, and Kay Steinmetz.

I further acknowledge the following:

Syracuse University Press for allowing me to reprint and/or adapt the recipes from my earlier book, *The Sensible Cook: Dutch Foodways in the Old and the New World*, as well as reprint some of the advice for cooking with children from *Childhood Pleasures: Dutch Children in the Seventeenth Century*.

The Overlook Press for allowing me to adapt the general instructions for fireplace cooking from my earlier book, *Foods of the Hudson*.

Mrs. Robert P. Browne and Historic Hudson Valley, Tarrytown, NY, for allowing me to use the De Peyster-van Cortlandt cookery manuscript (Mss VA 2444) and the Douw-Stevenson cookbook (Mss VA 2443).

Finally, I would like to express my deep love for my husband Don, who patiently listens to my stories and helps me in every way possible, and for my daughter Peter Pamela Rose, who is a wonderful cook, but above all a wonderful person.

Introduction

IT SEEMS THAT HISTORICAL FOOD is often thought of as unappetizing, or a gray glop. With these recipes I hope to prove to you that the contrary is true. Many are adapted from *De Verstandige Kock* (The Sensible Cook), the definitive Dutch cookbook of the seventeenth century, in its role as a component of the larger work *Het Vermakelijck Landtleven* (The Pleasurable Country Life). The anonymously written *De Verstandige Kock* was first published by Marcus Doornick in 1667. Including its two appendixes, "De Hollantse Slacht-tijdt" (The Dutch Butchering Time) and "De Verstandige Confituur-maker" (The Sensible Confectioner), it was later incorporated into *Het Vermakelijck Landtleven*. Unless otherwise attributed, all quotations are from the 1683 edition of this work, again published by Marcus Doornick. This collective work was a very useful book for owners of country homes and it is highly likely that Dutch settlers or descendants had it sent from the homeland; we know from remaining correspondence this was something they were wont to do. There are many copies of the book (published until the beginning of the nineteenth century) in libraries all over America.

In many cases, I have used modern versions of the recipes in *De Verstandige Kock* reprinted or adapted from my earlier book, *The Sensible Cook: Dutch Foodways in the Old and the New World*. Where necessary the recipes have been slightly modified for better understanding in the new context. Every recipe that I have tried from *De Verstandige Kock* has worked and delighted with its imaginative preparation of familiar foods.

My aim has been to make the recipes accessible to everyone, not only historical cooks, although I have included a few recipes, mostly for their historical interest. I am a hands-on culinary historian and like to know how dishes were prepared at the time that the recipes were written. Over the years I have taken courses in hearth cooking and have had great fun trying out many of the dishes in our home fireplace. Ours is large (48 inches wide × 38 inches high × 18 inches deep), but the "General Instructions for Fireplace Cooking" (see below) will make clear that you can prepare some food in a fireplace of almost any size. We learned how to do it the hard way. After some burned pots, some messy spills, and a few blisters, we are now rather good at fixing a meal over the fire with a minimum amount of fuss or mess.

Fireplace cooking is most fun if you have a partner. One of you is the cook; the other tends the fire. For us the choice is easy. My husband is known for his spectacular, carefully built fires. We have a great time cooking together, solving problems as we go along. Foods, especially breads, cooked at the hearth have an irresistible flavor.

When dinner is served, we eat by candlelight and the light of the fire and grin conspiratorially at each other while we taste our latest creation. Afterwards, as we enjoy the last of our wine, we sometimes companionably nod off. It is a relaxing and fun way to spend a winter's evening.

Whether you cook over fire or on the stove, the recipes will surprise and, I hope, enchant you. The buttered chestnuts, the Brabant stew with ginger, the baked cod with mace, the waffles, the New Year's cakes with caraway and orange zest, and the fruit-filled raised pies are only some of the dishes bringing an intriguing taste of the past!

PLEASE NOTE:
Both cookies and sweet or savory raised pies can be baked on the fire in a Dutch oven. I did not mark those recipes with a flame for fireplace cooking, because I see cookie baking as a great project to do with children in the kitchen and the raised pies as a more advanced fireplace baking project that you will tackle once more experience has been obtained. Please read the following instructions carefully.

General Instructions for Fireplace Cooking

Safety first. Have your chimney cleaned and checked on a regular basis. If possible, wear woolen clothing, which smolders rather than burns. Avoid synthetics; even when treated they flare quickly. Keep hair tied back and out of the way.

Food takes about the same time to cook over the fire as it does on the kitchen stove, once you have learned how to manage a fire. It is not harmed at all by standing in a warm place, waiting to be served, so there is no need to feel anxious or rushed if it is done sooner than you expected. Nor is there need for anxiety if it takes longer; the cooking itself is part of the fun. Therefore, only invite those friends to fireplace meals who can get into the spirit of the occasion.

Almost anything you can do on the stove or in the oven can be done in the fireplace, providing you have the equipment. When cooking simple dishes in the fireplace, braising, stewing, and other cooking techniques involving lots of liquid are the easiest. For baking use the Dutch oven. The dishes in this book that are particularly suited to fireplace cooking have been marked with a flame symbol 🔥.

You might be tempted to use the charcoal grill or hibachi indoors. This is safe only when the grill is placed in a fireplace with a proper upward draft. You need to be very careful about carbon monoxide fumes when using a charcoal grill indoors. I would not recommend doing so.

About an hour before you plan to start cooking, build a fire in one corner of the fireplace and replenish it with wood as it burns down. This fire will supply the embers that will produce a long-lasting, steady heat source. Hardwoods such as ash or oak work well and fruit and nut woods are particularly good. Avoid soft woods, such as pine, which produce creosote. They make the pots hard to clean and give the food a nasty flavor.

Just remember that the food is not cooked over flames but over coals extracted from the fire you built. These coals will glow at first, then turn gray as they cool, but they will keep their heat for a long time. When you have a good supply of coals, take several shovelfuls and create as many "burners" as you need by heaping the embers in small piles on the floor of the fireplace, away from the main fire. The cooking pots are set over these "burners." If you are using a pot with legs, set it right over the coals. If not, place the pot on a trivet set over the coals. Lacking a trivet, stack two bricks on either side of the coals and put the pot on them.

The equipment needed for fireplace cooking is quite minimal. Other than an old pot or two and some trivets or bricks, all you need are oven mitts and a long-handled fork and spoon. My husband and I now have acquired a very handy lid-lifting gadget which stabilizes the lid while removing it. You might be able to find this and other items useful for fireplace cooking at tag sales, flea markets, and hardware and camping goods stores.

Historically, roasting was done on a spit in front of the fire, or in a tin oven, sometimes called a reflector oven or even Dutch oven. Used in front of the fireplace, not in it, the tin oven contains a spit for meat, which cooks by heat reflected from the fire on the oven's inner walls. It gives delicious results. Unfortunately, we found that it is just a little too easy to get spills on the living room carpet, so we no longer use our tin oven indoors. We do use a true Dutch oven, which looks like a large cast-iron pan with a flat lid on which coals are heaped.

Some Dutch ovens have concave lids; these pots are buried in the coals; we prefer the flat-lidded type. When preheated, the Dutch oven becomes a fireplace-oven in which we bake our bread. Keep in mind that bread-baking requires more heat on top than on the bottom.

Although most cast-iron ware has been pre-seasoned to resist sticking, for liquid-based cooking it is advisable nonetheless to season the utensil before first use. Wash it with soap and water and dry completely. Coat the inside with unsalted fat (preferably suet) or vegetable oil and place it in a slow (300°F) oven for about 3 hours.

Turn off the oven and let the pan cool completely, then wipe off excess fat with paper towels. It is a miserable, smelly job, but it must be done to prevent your pots from rusting. Fortunately, you only have to do it once! Another solution is to buy aluminum pots, which are lighter and require no seasoning. If you use your everyday pans for fireplace cooking, borrow the old scout trick of soaping the exterior. This will prevent the soot from sticking. Clean with a soapy steel wool pad.

PLEASE NOTE:

The recipes are for 4 people unless otherwise indicated.

Salted butter is used throughout because that is what was used originally. If you prefer to use unsalted butter, use the following formula: Add ¼ teaspoon salt per stick (½ cup) of unsalted butter.

History on Our Plate

Dutch Foodways

An American Connection

Overview of Dutch Culinary History from the Middle Ages until the Seventeenth Century

THE EARLIEST PRINTED COOKBOOK in the Dutch language, *Een Notabel Boecxken van Cokeryen* (A Notable Little Book of Cookery), was published circa 1514. The presumed author and publisher, Thomas van der Noot, belonged to a prominent Brussels family. Van der Noot's book was meant for the nobility, high-placed clergy, and wealthy bourgeoisie, for only these classes could afford the expensive foodstuffs it called for. As was common practice then, many of the 170 or so recipes were copied from other sources, especially from the famous French cookbook of the period, *Le Viandier. Een Notabel Boecxken van Cokeryen* includes recipes for sauces, fish dishes, meats, poultry, game, and eggs, as well as for raised pies, tarts, and sweets. The recipes are clearly divided into dishes for everyday consumption and those to be eaten on the church-ordained days of fasting and abstinence, when meat, dairy products, and eggs were forbidden. This prohibition applied to about 150 days a year, when only fish, vegetables, herbs, fruits (including dried fruits and nuts), legumes, oils, salt, spices, sugar, honey, beer, wine, grain products, and bread were permitted. These rules were far more stringent than the ones American Roman Catholics practiced until the mid-1960s.

Eggs, said to be the poor man's supper, were particularly popular in the Netherlands. They were often barely cooked and then slurped from the shell.

During the Middle Ages, milk was not drunk as it is today, in part because it spoiled quickly and was thought to be unhealthy, so much so that after drinking it one was advised to rinse one's mouth with honey! Instead it was cooked in porridges, or custards, some of which had a pastry base.

Milk was also preserved as butter and as the less perishable cheese. In the Low Countries, unlike other parts of Europe, butter rather than oil was used. Several varieties of cheese, made from both cows' and sheep's milk, were being manufactured as early as the fourteenth and fifteenth centuries. Cheese was usually named for the place where it originated; the Netherlands is still known for its Gouda and Edam cheeses. Gouda cheese is made from milk with cream and Edam-style cheese is made from skimmed milk. Early on, sheep cheeses were also popular. Often colored green with sheep's feces, these cheeses primarily came from the northern island of Texel or the town of 's Gravenzande. As breeding methods improved and milk production increased, more recipes appeared for milk products, including home-made ricotta-like cheeses.

Pork was the favorite meat of all classes. Pigs were everywhere and generally roamed free. In the fall, pigs were slaughtered, and families who could afford it would purchase a cow for slaughter as well. Both were salted and smoked for winter consumption. By the end of the sixteenth century, cattle, particularly oxen, were imported from Denmark and Schleswig-Holstein in northern Germany, to be fattened for slaughter in the grassy meadows of the northern Netherlands. Chickens, ducks, and geese were the common poultry, although songbirds were eaten as well.

The nobility had the privilege of hunting both large and small game animals, including deer, wild boar, rabbits, pheasants, partridge, bittern, cranes, swans, heron, and ducks. Falcons and sparrow hawks were trained to retrieve partridge, geese, ducks, kites, and doves, or any other fowl. By the fifteenth century, game was usually reserved for feasts rather than the daily table of the noblemen.

It is often implied that medieval people strongly seasoned their foods because meat was generally spoiled, an unlikely premise since many government regulations concerned the sale of meat and people knew about preservation methods like drying, smoking, and salting. Seasoning was, as it is now, more a matter of taste. Spices from the Orient, such as pepper, nutmeg, cloves, and cinnamon, were introduced by way of Venice and became status symbols for the well-to-do. These spices were mixed with sour verjuice (juice from unripe grapes or apples) and locally grown herbs such as parsley, sage, or savory. They gave the dishes a sharply spiced and sour taste, which was much appreciated.

Little is known about the sustenance of the masses in the Middle Ages, since the body of knowledge about food of the period comes from records of the elaborate banquets held by the nobility for weddings, victories, or coronations. These extravagant medieval feasts consisted of several courses, each containing ten or more dishes, and were also known for their between-course events. At one of Philip of Burgundy's banquets, an entire orchestra stepped out of a raised pie and started to play!

Fishing was as important to the food supply as it was to the economy. In the fifteenth century, when large schools of herring moved closer to the Netherlands, the Dutch herring fishery boomed. The invention of *haring kaken* (the cleaning and salting of herring on board ship) made the fish less perishable and therefore available as a major trade good. Salt, also used to preserve meat, was imported from France and Portugal. Herring and dried cod were the chief fish eaten by all Dutch classes and were especially important on days of fasting and abstinence. Eel were abundant in the rivers, as were carp, pike, and bream. These freshwater fish were preferred by the more affluent, while the poor and working class ate dried plaice, flounder, or whiting.

Castles and cloisters were the centers of horticulture at the beginning of the Middle Ages, and their gardens provided vegetables, herbs, fruits, and nuts. Gradually, however, the increased mercantile influence of the large towns (such as Antwerp and Amsterdam) and their expanding markets allowed horticulture to begin to flourish beyond the estates of the nobility and clergy. By the sixteenth century, the Netherlands was known throughout Europe for its vegetables. To extend the growing season, seeds were cultivated under glass in cold frames. In 1556, Gheeraert Vorselman's *Een Nyeuwen Coock Boeck* (A New Cookbook) was the first to publish salad and vegetable recipes. For some of his recipes he too drew on older works such as Platina's *Honesta Volupta* and also Taillevent's *Viandier*.

In the Middle Ages wheat, rye, barley, oats, peas, and beans were grown. However, the Netherlands did not grow enough grain to supply its inhabitants, so large quantities of grain were imported, mostly from eastern Prussia and Poland. The grain trade developed early, and by the fifteenth century it was concentrated in Amsterdam. Bread was one of the mainstays of the diet. The more expensive wheat bread (called white bread) was eaten by the affluent and was sometimes referred to as "*herenbrood*" or "gentleman's bread." Dark rye bread was the usual food of the poor.

Beer was the common drink, although wine was favored by the well-to-do and buttermilk was popular on the farms. Beer was brewed at home, but as early as the fourteenth century, the cities of Haarlem and Amersfoort had famous breweries. Cloisters, too, were known for their brews and some of the famous present-day Belgian beers date back to that tradition.

Abundant feasts at times of plenty contrasted with the famines of the Middle Ages, which wiped out large parts of the population. The Dutch were true trenchermen, who would eat and drink immoderately at parties and banquets for guild celebrations, weddings, or births (where they would "drown the child" in frequent toasts), or at funerals (called in jest "grave weddings"). Paintings by Breughel and other artists of the period depict such events.

However, the regular meal pattern consisted, at most, of two meals a day, with two dishes for the main meal served around eleven in the morning and one dish for the evening meal, served just before going to bed. Bread, cheese, root vegetables, garlic, onions, peas, beans, fruit in season, porridge, eggs, and a little meat or fish, when available, were the main foodstuffs. Toward the end of the Middle Ages, mealtimes shifted and, increasingly, breakfast was added as the third meal of the day.

Before all meals hands were washed, for which a water pitcher, bowl, and towel or napkin were provided. Plates were first dried slices of bread, replaced by wooden trenchers and eventually tin dishes. The table was covered with a cloth with bread and salt placed upon it. Fingers, spoons, or knives were used for eating. Forks were not used until the end of the seventeenth century.

A major change in eating habits occurred in the middle of the sixteenth century, after the Protestant Reformation, when the northern provinces of the Netherlands largely embraced the Protestant faith, as preached by John Calvin, and the southern provinces remained Roman Catholic. It may be assumed that the Protestants abandoned the days of abstinence early on, although they continued to eat fish on Friday. The Catholic obligation to fast was difficult and expensive, causing some medievalists to believe this could be one of the reasons for the success of the Reformation. It is worth noting that most olive oil-producing countries remained Catholic and most butter-producing countries became Protestant.

Food and Drink in the Netherlands during the Seventeenth Century

Daily Meals and Customary Beverages

The seventeenth century brought the great prosperity known as the "Golden Age." Both the East and West India Companies were founded in its first quarter, allowing Dutch ships to bring spices from the Dutch East Indies (now Indonesia) and sugar from first Brazil and then plantations in the West Indies. Exotic plants, such as the pineapple, were brought from every port where Dutch ships docked. With more food available, consumption increased and the common eating pattern grew to four meals a day. Breakfast consisted of bread with butter or cheese, perhaps a *sop*, or vegetable stew, and meat if available; the noon meal consisted of a stew of meat and vegetables or of fish, with fruit, cooked vegetables, honey cake, or raised pie and bread. The afternoon meal of bread with butter or cheese was eaten a few hours later and was more of a snack. Just before bedtime, leftovers from noon, or bread with butter or cheese, or porridge was served.

The Dutch were known for their love of sweets, sweet breads like honey cake or ginger bread, and confections like marzipan, candied almonds, or cinnamon bark, which were consumed in addition to the daily fare. Like their cheeses, the Dutch *koek* (honey cake), akin to ginger bread, was named for its city of origin. By the fifteenth century, *Deventer koek* from the town of Deventer in the eastern Netherlands was already famous throughout the land. Waffles, wafers, *olie-koecken* (deep-fried balls of dough with raisins, apples, and almonds that became a forerunner of the donut), and pancakes were some of the celebratory foods both prepared at home and sold on the streets, as contemporary artists portray.

Beer continued to be the common drink and was served at all meals. Because water was boiled in its preparation, beer was a safer drink than plain water, which was frequently polluted. Buttermilk was often drunk on the farm. The sweeter and less perishable wines from the Mediterranean countries were popular with the upper classes. Young white wines, imported from France and Germany, were at that time very sour, so they were mixed with honey and spices such as cloves, coriander, cinnamon, and ginger to make a sweet drink like *hippocras*, which was enjoyed by the upper classes at the end of a large meal (see recipes).

In the latter half of the seventeenth century tea and coffee made a significant impact on meal patterns and social customs. An early tea cargo in 1610 was considered a curiosity, but shipments gradually increased and domestic markets developed. Tea preparation required its own paraphernalia such as small porcelain tea bowls and teapots, also imported from the Orient. Many humorous tales exist about the quantity consumed at popular late seventeenth-century tea parties, where purportedly between twenty and one hundred small cupfuls per person were drunk. Tea was served with sweets such as hard candies, marzipan, and cookies, particularly a Utrecht specialty called *theerandjes* (literally, "tea edges," or strips), made from a clove-flavored dough topped with candied orange peel and citron (see recipes). The third meal of the day (snack), which earlier in the century had consisted of bread and butter, was incorporated into the tea ritual and moved to the late afternoon.

During teatime, women would gather in small groups, which had a certain cachet. Coffee, however, was a more public drink. It was enjoyed in coffeehouses, where men would stop in to have a cup, smoke a pipe, and read the paper. Stephanus Blankaart, an Amsterdam physician and author of the 1633 book on diet, *De Burgerlyke Tafel Om Lang Gesond Zonder Ziekten te Leven* (The Bourgeois Table to Live Long without Illnesses), comments on the large crowds visiting the coffeehouses in his city.

Diet of the Poor and Working Class

The poor had a much more limited diet. In some parts of the country daily meals consisted of not much more than whole kernel rye (black) bread, amounting to some five pounds a day for a family of four. The remarkably complete account books of the Amsterdam Municipal Orphanage provide more insight into the diet of the poor (the orphans), and the working or lower middle class (the staff). Milk, fish, rice, groats (hulled grain of barley, oats, or buckwheat), peas, beans, rye, wheat, pork, butter, cheese, beer, and miscellaneous items such as treacle, salt, dried fruits, and spices were purchased for their daily meals. As noted in the menu for the year 1640, the orphans were fed two meals a day. The noon meal consisted of different varieties of beans and peas and a second dish of salted or smoked meat, or sausage with groats and raisins, bacon with carrots or cabbage, salt cod, herring, or dried cod. All of the meals were served with bread (and beer). The evening repast invariably consisted of a kind of porridge such as rice porridge, groats cooked with buttermilk, buttermilk with rye bread, bread and treacle cooked together, buttermilk and wheat bread cooked together, or buttermilk cooked with barley. The main difference between the diets of the orphans and the staff was quantity. The adult staff was given more bread (especially wheat bread) and more meat.

Diet of the Wealthy Middle and Upper Classes

With fortunes made in overseas trade, well-to-do families built country houses away from their city dwellings and places of business. The country houses had gardens where fruits and vegetables were grown for home consumption, a "not bought feast" or *dapes inemptae* as it was called in several odes to their gardens by proud homeowners. Plants from faraway lands were also cultivated.

While some ten books and manuscripts, including *Een Notabel Boecxken van Cokeryen,* were printed in the southern Netherlands, within the current boundaries of the Netherlands, only a few books were printed before the definitive Dutch cookbook of the seventeenth century, the anonymously written *De Verstandige Kock* (The Sensible Cook). I included a translation of *De Verstandige Kock* in my book *The Sensible Cook: Dutch Foodways in the Old and the New World* (Syracuse University Press, 1989 and 1998). Originally incorporated into a book on gardening by Pieter van Aengelen and published by Marcus Doornick in 1667, *De Verstandige Kock* later formed part of a larger collective book, *Het Vermakelijck Landtleven* (The Pleasurable Country Life). Its only actual forerunner was *Eenen Seer Schonen/ende Excellenten Cockboeck* (A Very Beautiful/and Excellent Cookbook) written by Carolus Battus and published in 1589. Some of its recipes were copied in *De Verstandige Kock*, as was a common practice at the time.

Unless otherwise attributed, all recipes and quotations in this book are taken from the 1683 edition of *De Verstandige Kock*, also published by Marcus Doornick.

The collective work *Het Vermakelijck Landtleven* contains a wealth of information on gardening, orchards, beekeeping, herbs, distilling, medicines, food preservation and, through *De Verstandige Kock*, cooking of the period. It is highly probable that if Dutch settlers of the last quarter of the seventeenth century brought over any books this book was among them. It is even more likely that copies of the book were ordered from the Netherlands as we know settlers and descendants were wont to do well into the eighteenth century. At the present time there are many copies in libraries all across America.

De Verstandige Kock gives recipes for the homegrown bounty of the country estates of the rising middle and upper classes. Like the cookbooks of previous centuries, it was written for this rapidly expanding wealthy upper class, which had become the leading segment of Dutch society as the power of the nobility waned. *De Verstandige Kock* begins with salads and continues with recipes for vegetables, meat, game, and poultry, salted, smoked, and dried fish, saltwater and freshwater fish, and baked goods such as raised pies and tarts. Separate chapters on preserving meats and fruits end the volume. The book gives the impression that the daily fare of the wealthy was plentiful and varied.

Bread as the Mainstay of the Diet

Bread was consumed with butter or cheese for breakfast, was paired with meat or *hutspot* (a one-pot dish of meats and vegetables) for the midday main meal, was the main item of the afternoon snack, and was served with, or a part of, the porridge at night. Special baked goods followed the human life cycle, from *zottinnekoecken* (pastries akin to rusks; literally, "crazy woman's cakes" or "airhead" cakes for their light texture), which were served filled with sugared comfits for celebrations of births, to *doot coeckjes*, or funeral cookies, the recipe for which appears in the manuscript cookbook of Maria Sanders van Rensselaer (1749–1830), wife of Philip van Rensselaer of Cherry Hill, Albany. In the seventeenth century the poor and working class continued to eat rye or coarse wheat bread; daily consumption of white bread was a symbol of affluence.

Rye and wheat were the main grain ingredients for bread baking in the Netherlands. Rye, grown in the drier eastern and southern provinces, produced a dark (black) bread. Wheat, mostly imported, produced a lighter bread with softer crumb, or, when sifted, a finely textured white bread. In the workroom, often behind his shop, the baker mixed the flour, salt, yeast, and water into dough, which was then kneaded to the right consistency. Wheat dough was kneaded by hand; the heavier rye dough was kneaded in a trough with the feet. By government regulation, hands or feet were not to be washed with soap, but with hot water, then rubbed with flour.

Bread dough was shaped in various ways and sometimes flavored with nutmeg, cloves, and especially cinnamon, or filled with dried fruits and decorated with sugar, or even gold leaf. Each baker also placed his own identification mark on his products. It was not the bakers who set the price for their bread, but the local government. Part of a government's task was to ensure sufficient food was available to protect the population from famine. Seventeenth-century municipal governments regulated the size, weight, and price of bread by appointing inspectors to oversee its production. Bread prices were established in relation to grain prices. Rye bread had stable weights of six and twelve pounds, but its price would vary (*zetting*). For white bread, the price would be stable, but the weight would vary (*rijding*). Prices and weights were announced in bulletins affixed to prominent structures in town.

Bakers were organized into guilds, which petitioned the government on behalf of their membership and regulated and curtailed the bakers' trade. These necessary restrictions ensured an adequate market share for each bakery. To be a full member of the baker's guild, one had to be a citizen of the town, complete an apprenticeship, and pass the baker's exam.

Food and Drink in New Netherland

Every day Americans eat dishes that can be traced back to the foodways brought to New Netherland (the present-day states of New York, New Jersey, and Delaware, and parts of Maryland, Pennsylvania, and Connecticut) by the early Dutch settlers, who planted fruit trees (among them apples, pears, and peaches), vegetables such as lettuces, cabbages, parsnips, carrots, and beets, and herbs such as parsley, rosemary, chives, and tarragon. Farm animals, particularly horses, pigs, and cows, were among the most valuable imported commodities.

Adriaen van der Donck, a graduate of the University of Leiden with a doctorate in civil and canon law, came to New Netherland in 1641 to become *schout* (sheriff) for Patroon Kiliaen van Rensselaer (c. 1585–1643) in Rensselaerswijck (now Albany and Rensselaer Counties). He wrote *A Description of the New Netherlands* (first published in 1655) to entice his fellow countrymen to settle in the new colony. Van der

Donck reported that all sorts of European fruits and vegetables "thrive well," and marveled at the abundance of native fish, fowl, and other wildlife (1968).

Trade with Native Americans was an important aspect of life in New Netherland. The Dutch traded cloth, beads, and ironware such as axes and cooking kettles for beaver skins and also used their baking skills to produce breads, sweet breads, and cookies as commodities. Native Americans valued Dutch wheat bread, which had been previously unknown to them. Whereas in the Netherlands most of the wheat was imported, in the Rensselaerswijck *patroonship*, wheat became the most important cash crop. Evidently bakers were using so much flour for the lucrative Indian trade that not enough was left to bake bread for the Dutch community. A 1649 ordinance for Fort Orange and the village of Beverwijck (now Albany) forbade further baking of bread and cookies for Native Americans. There was even a record of a court case in which a baker was fined because "a certain savage" was seen coming out of his house "carrying an oblong sugar bun." At mid-century, the bakers signed a petition to organize a guild, but they were denied, and no guilds were ever established in New Netherland.

In their new colony, the settlers continued to prepare familiar foods. From ship records we know that West India Company ships supplied them with kitchen tools, such as frying pans to fry their favorite pancakes, or the irons to make their waffles and wafers (see recipes). As diaries and inventories note, the settlers duplicated life in the Netherlands as best as they could. Cookbooks of their descendants show that they continued their own foodways but also incorporated native foods into their daily diet, albeit in ways that were familiar to them. For instance, they made pumpkin cornmeal pancakes or pumpkin sweetmeat, or added cranberries instead of the usual raisins and apples to their favorite *olie-koecken*. Lovers of porridge found it easy to get used to *sapaen* (Indian cornmeal mush), but they added milk to it. This dish became such an integral part of the Dutch American diet that it is mentioned under the heading of "National Dishes" on an 1830 menu for the Saint Nicholas' Day Dinner held at the American Hotel in Albany. Cookies, pancakes, waffles, wafers, *olie-koecken*, pretzels, and coleslaw are some of the recipes that were brought to America by the Dutch colonists. While the Dutch period of New Netherland only lasted officially from 1609 to 1664, the Dutch influence, particularly the culinary influence, persists to this day.

Foods for Special Occasions in the Netherlands and New Netherland

The seventeenth-century Dutch celebrated four winter holidays: Saint Nicholas' Day on December sixth, but later celebrated on the eve of that day (the evening of December 5 is still a big occasion for family celebrations and gift giving in the Netherlands), Christmas, New Year's, and Epiphany (Twelfth Night, or the Feast of the Three Kings) on January sixth. For children, Saint Nicholas' Day was the most important, and the traditions from this celebration have been absorbed into our American Christmas festivities. Virtually nothing is certain about the real Saint Nicholas. His legend may have grown out of life stories of several bishops by that name. According to tradition, he was a fourth-century bishop of Myra, in Asia Minor, who became associated with anonymous gift-giving. Saint Nicholas was also the patron saint of sailors, who brought his cult via the sea routes from Eastern to Western Europe. In the Low Countries, he was often the main character in the miracle plays performed in town squares. This made him less a venerated saint and more of a popular figure. He became the *kindervriend*, or children's friend, who brought presents and sweet treats to the small folk. The latter included *duivekaters* (holiday bread), candied cinnamon bark, or flat, chewy honey cake formed in a wooden mold. He was so much a part of yearly family celebrations that even during the Reformation the *Kinderfeest* (children's feast) could not be eradicated by government and Protestant church officials and the celebration has lasted until this day.

In the beginning of the nineteenth century, the American novelist Washington Irving (1783–1859), observing the Saint Nicholas' Day celebrations by his Dutch American neighbors, borrowed its central figure and made him part of the American Christmas festivities. He changed the tall, thin, stern-but-just bishop into our short, rotund, and jolly Santa Claus. Nineteenth-century illustrators created further embellishments to his appearance, while different ethnic groups added their traditions, and the result was the secular component of the American Christmas celebration.

In the Netherlands, the religious holidays such as Christmas, Easter, and Pentecost were (and still are) celebrated for two days. Deacons' records of the Dutch Reformed Church show they were celebrated this way in New Netherland as well.

New Year's Eve was especially noisy, with the firing of guns to bring in the New Year. Ordinances in both the Netherlands and New Netherland eventually prohibited such behavior. The special treat for New Year's Day in the Netherlands was *nieuwjaarskoeken* (thin, crisp wafers), which originated in the eastern part of the country and adjoining parts of Germany. These wafers were made in a special wafer iron. The oblong or round long-handled irons, made by blacksmiths, created imprints of a religious or secular nature on the wafers. Wafer irons were often given as a wedding gift, even in this country. Enormous quantities of wafers were prepared on New Year's Day. They were consumed by family, servants, and guests and distributed to children, who went from house to house singing New Year's songs, while collecting their share of treats along the way. There is ample evidence in diaries and letters that Dutch Americans continued the custom of visiting each other on New Year's Day. In New Netherland, however, the *nieuwjaarskoeken* were molded in wooden cake-boards, instead of wafer irons (see recipes in the manuscript cookbooks of Elizabeth Ann Breese Morse [d. 1828] and Maria Lott Lefferts [1786–1865] of Brooklyn). The American New Year's cake is a combination of two Dutch pastries brought here by the early settlers, the *nieuwjaarskoeken* described above and spiced, chewy, honey cakes formed in a wooden mold or cake-board. It was in the late eighteenth century that this homemade pastry prepared in heirloom wafer irons by the Dutch changed to a mostly store-bought product purchased by the population at large. Bakers found it much more expedient to roll out the dough, imprint it with a cake-board, cut it out, and bake it. Because the pastry was not connected with a religious celebration, most groups easily adopted it.

Culinary historian Stephen Schmidt holds that Americans became acquainted with Dutch cookies through *nieuwjaarskoeken* (New Year's cakes), bringing the word *cookie* into American English. Recipes for cookies appeared for the first time in the earliest published American cookbook, compiled by Amelia Simmons in 1796. Cake-boards developed into a unique kind of folk art, similar to their counterparts in the Netherlands, recording important events of the time, political figures, or the American eagle.

The last Dutch winter holiday, Epiphany, did not leave a lasting mark on American life. In the Netherlands it was a rather rowdy occasion, celebrated within the family circle with waffles and pancakes served as the standard fare.

The spring religious feast of Easter was celebrated in some parts of the Netherlands with large bonfires and most everywhere with the consumption of Easter eggs. No specific mention of Easter (other than the collection of offerings by the deacons of the Dutch Reformed Church) has been found in New Netherland.

Pinkster, Pentecost, or Whitsuntide, the third most important holiday in the Christian calendar, which occurs fifty days after Easter, was celebrated in the Netherlands as well as in New Netherland. In the Old World, the secular festivities associated with *Pinksteren*, as it is now called, were a kind of combined May Day and fertility celebration. To foster a good harvest, a young girl was chosen as the *Pinksterblom* (*Pinkster* flower) and was carried around bedecked with flowers by the children of the town, who collected coins to buy treats. New Netherland diaries relate how the Dutch settlers gave their slaves the day off and everyone frolicked and ate large quantities of eggs. After the Revolution and in the beginning of the nineteenth century, the holiday tended to be more and more a celebration for African Americans. New York City, where freed slaves had arrived in large numbers, was especially known for its lavish *Pinkster* festivals, and in Albany *Pinkster* is said to have lasted a whole week. As an interesting aside, in his article "Pinkster Carnival: Africanisms in the Hudson River Valley," Professor A. J. Williams-Myers of SUNY New Paltz, NY, asserts that as a result of the *Pinkster* festivals "for almost two hundred years some forms of

Africanisms were able to survive within the institution of slavery in New York. . . . These were passed on from generation to generation, from Old World African to New World African, so that by the nineteenth century Pinkster carnival had become an African celebration" (*Afro-Americans in New York Life and History* 9 (1985): 7–17).

In both the Netherlands and New Netherland, there were many additional events associated with special foods. These include yearly fairs, where waffles, wafers, and *olie-koecken* were sold; the birth of a child, with its special drink of *kandeel* (wine with eggs and spices; see recipes); and weddings, where guests feasted on the best the household had to offer. That even funerals were part of the well-defined culinary customs of the colony may be gleaned from the recipes for *doot coeckjes* (funeral cookies) and spiced wine of Maria Sanders van Rensselaer (1749–1830). At all festivities the Dutch proved to be truly hearty eaters. For example, a typical three-course feast to mark the accession to office of two Groningen professors featured turkey, hare, haunch of mutton, ham, veal, and half a lamb, all served with bread, butter, cheese, mustard, anchovies, lemons, and wine. It is telling, therefore, that Adriaen van der Donck, who served as sheriff in Rensselaerswijck, specifically noted that Native Americans "have no excessive eaters or gluttons among them" (1968).

Implements and Household Objects

Some of the common implements of a seventeenth-century kitchen included kettles, in various sizes and usually made from brass, which were hung over the fire and used for boiling water, or for cooking food in liquid. Cooking pots—tall, earthenware vessels with narrow necks— were also used for cooking with liquids (see book cover) and so were their bronze or brass successors. Braising or stewing pans were covered with a lid to trap the steam for cooking with a limited amount of liquid. Frying pans were used for cooking over high heat with a small amount of fat. A spit with dripping pan was used for roasting. A *taert-panne* (Dutch oven) served as a small portable oven for baking the sweet and savory raised pies and cookies. Its lipped lid allowed coals to be heaped on top so that the baked good(s) would be heated from above and below. The use of a gridiron, which was placed over hot coals to roast flat pieces of meat or fish or to toast bread to be grated and used to thicken sauces, is implied in some of the recipes (see recipes). The recipes for waffles and wafers require two kinds of irons. A rasp, sieve, colander, mortar and pestle, and skimmer, as well as knives and spoons, plates, platters, cups, glasses, bowls, pots, bottles, basins for storage, and a *vleeschkuyp* (a wooden tub for pickling meat) round out the implement list for a well-equipped seventeenth-century kitchen. At the end of the century the very wealthy began to furnish their guests with eating implements, including a knife and spoon and the newer fork. However, several decades elapsed before the fork was generally accepted; many people claimed it was unnecessary because, in the common phrase, "God has given us fingers."

Cookbooks

The cookbooks handed down in Dutch American families prove that the colonists maintained their familiar foodways for generations. Their recipes are found in manuscript cookbooks spanning more than three centuries. Close to forty such cookbooks, belonging to descendants of the Dutch settlers of New Netherland, who retained their culinary ethnicity by handing down their special recipes, have been identified.

From some of the families only a single book remains, such as the undated "Mrs. Lefferts' Book," handwritten by Maria Lott Lefferts (1786–1865) of Brooklyn, or that of Elizabeth Ann Breese Morse (d. 1828), entitled "Mrs. E. A. Morse, Her Book, April 10, 1805." Not surprisingly, the wealthiest families—the Van Cortlandts of the lower Hudson Valley, the Van Rensselaers of Albany, and the Dutch families in the New Paltz area—have left the richest assortment.

There are five Van Cortlandt manuscripts; the two most important belonged to Anna de Peyster (1701–74) and to Anne Stevenson van Cortlandt (1774–1821) and her mother, Magdalena Douw (1750–1817). The Van Rensselaer family was amazingly prolific in its record-keeping. Its members produced at least twelve manuscript cookbooks over five generations, spanning almost two hundred years. That of Maria Sanders van Rensselaer (1749–1830) is the earliest, followed by those of her daughter Arriet (1775–1840) and her granddaughter Elizabeth (1799–1835).

Manuscripts of lesser-known families have also survived. A manuscript by Anna Maria Elting of New Paltz is dated May 18, 1819. "Hylah Hasbrouck's Receipts," now in the archives of Young-Morse Historic Site in Poughkeepsie, NY, and dated 1840, includes a recipe for *condale*, or *kandeel*, the customary drink celebrating the birth of a child, as do several of the other manuscript cookbooks. Hybertie Pruyn (1873–1964) of Albany and even Washington Irving had several Dutch recipes among their papers.

In this span of three hundred and fifty years, recipes changed, partially because the fine details of the methods were forgotten, but also because modern equipment replaced old utensils, or new ingredients were used. Not only did the recipes evolve, but also their names became more and more Anglicized. *Krullen* (curls), a curl-shaped deep-fried pastry, became *crulla* or *crullar*, and ended up as today's cruller. In the handwritten cookbooks, waffles are frequently spelled phonetically in Dutch as *wafuls*. Another good example is coleslaw. The origin of this cabbage salad is apparently completely forgotten, yet the name comes simply from the Dutch *kool* for cabbage, and *sla* for slaw or salad. The widest variety of spellings found was for the seventeenth century *olie-koecken* (oil cakes), a word that has changed even in the Netherlands, where the pastry is now called *oliebollen* (oil-balls). The Dutch American spelling ranges from *oelykoeks* or *ollykoeks*, through *ole cook* to *oly cook* (see recipes for two versions).

Conclusion

To answer questions on how seventeenth-century foods actually tasted, please try the recipes that follow. In addition to adapted recipes from *De Verstandige Kock*, some extra recipes have been added to complete the story of Dutch foodways. The recipes make it possible for today's cook to serve up intriguing and enticing tastes of the past.

The Recipes

Salads & Vegetables

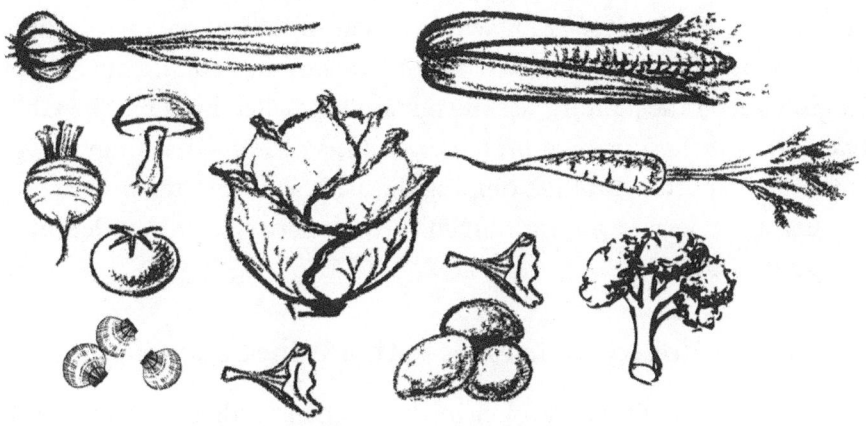

THE RECIPES IN THIS CHAPTER are simple and allow the vegetables to speak for themselves. Many are modernized versions of recipes found in the 1683 edition of the anonymously written *De Verstandige Kock* (The Sensible Cook), in its role as a component of the larger work *Het Vermakelijck Landtleven* (The Pleasurable Country Life); some remain standards in the Dutch kitchen today. The dishes marked with a small flame symbol are particularly suitable for fireplace cooking.

Asparagus with Butter & Egg Sauce

Nowadays in the Netherlands, asparagus is usually prepared in a simple manner and often served with salmon or meat. However, the following recipe gives an old-fashioned Dutch way of serving it by combining the vegetable with nutmeg, melted butter, and hard-boiled eggs.

1 pound asparagus, woody ends snapped off
Salt to taste
Freshly grated nutmeg
8 tablespoons (1 stick) melted salted butter
2 to 4 hard-boiled eggs

Steam the asparagus until tender, then lightly season it with salt. Place it on a platter, grating it liberally with nutmeg and drizzling it with a little of the melted butter. Arrange hard-boiled eggs, peeled and cut in half lengthwise, on the platter. Pass the remaining melted butter at the table. Each diner makes his own little sauce on his plate by mashing the egg with melted butter and then dipping the asparagus into the mixture.

For a modern vegetarian lunch or dinner, serve with boiled little red potatoes.

Boiled Artichokes with a Wine Sauce

Artichokes were already grown in the kitchen gardens of New Netherland in the seventeenth century (the present-day states of New York, New Jersey, and Delaware, and parts of Maryland, Pennsylvania, and Connecticut). Now our supplies come from fields in the temperate climate of California's Monterey County.

Try the following recipe for artichokes with a sauce of wine, bread crumbs, and cinnamon. They are a bit messy to eat, but quite worth it. The original in *De Verstandige Kock* reads: "They [the artichokes] are also stewed with crumbs from a stale white bread which has been soaked in red wine, finely mashed, and then a little vinegar added and sugar, cinnamon, nutmeg, pepper, and butter as appropriate."

1 large artichoke for two people, boiled until the bottom
can be pierced with a fork, 20 to 35 minutes, depending on size
⅓ cup plain, dry bread crumbs, briefly soaked in 1 cup dry
red wine
1 tablespoon wine vinegar
1½ teaspoon sugar
1 teaspoon ground cinnamon

¼ teaspoon EACH freshly grated nutmeg and ground pepper

4 tablespoons salted butter

In a saucepan large enough to hold the boiled artichoke (see above), combine soaked bread crumbs, vinegar, seasonings, and butter; heat until the butter is melted. Add the artichoke; cover the pan and gently stew a few minutes, stirring occasionally.

De Cierlijcke Voorsnijdinge Aller Tafel Gerechten (The Elegant Carving of all Dishes on the Table), a period book on etiquette and carving published in 1664, has the following serving suggestion. With a slotted spoon remove the artichoke to a plate or platter. Hold the artichoke upright with a fork and push the outer leaves down in a circle, so that it looks "like a rose." Remove the choke and inner leaves. Cut the heart into wedges. Serve each person some of the heart and outer leaves, along with a spoonful of sauce for scooping with the leaves.

For a modern meal, serve warm as a first course for two people.

Boiled Chestnuts

Chestnuts, simply boiled and seasoned with a little salt and melted butter, make such a delicious side dish that it is astonishing that chestnuts have gone out of fashion and are now used only to stuff the occasional goose. In his mid-sixteenth-century cookbook, *Een Nyeuwen Coock Boeck* (A New Cookbook), Gheeraert Vorselman suggests sprinkling boiled chestnuts with some sugar and cinnamon before serving. It is an idea worth trying.

1 pound chestnuts

4 tablespoons salted butter

Salt to taste

(2 tablespoons sugar mixed with 1½ teaspoons ground cinnamon, optional—see above)

Cut an X in the flat side of each chestnut. Place in a saucepan, or a pan suited for fireplace cooking, and cover with boiling water. Prepare a "burner," as described in "General Instructions for Fireplace Cooking" (pp. xiii–xv). Boil gently for about 15 minutes, or until shells and skin can easily be removed. Drain the chestnuts and cool until you are able to handle them, but keep them warm or they will not peel. Remove shells and skins. Wash out the pan, place the butter in it and melt over low heat. Return the chestnuts to the pan, reheat and season with salt. Shake the pan frequently to prevent burning; do not allow the butter to brown. If you would like to try this, mix sugar and cinnamon and sprinkle this mixture on the cooked chestnuts. Combine and serve.

For a modern meal, serve as a side dish. This is particularly good with pork, turkey, duck, or goose.

Braised Fava, Green, or Pole Beans

The original recipe in *De Verstandige Kock* reads: "Take fava or Turkish [green] beans cut up. When they are cooked until done, then drained, take chopped parsley with butter and salt, a spoonful or two of mutton broth, add them together in a pot so it can cook a bit, then add the beans, shake often. Sometimes some savory is also added, everyone to his own desire."

> 4 pounds fava beans (weighed while in the pods); or 1 pound green beans; or 1 pound pole beans
>
> 2 cups water
>
> 2 tablespoons lamb or beef broth
>
> 2 tablespoons salted butter
>
> 2 tablespoons chopped parsley
>
> 2 tablespoons fresh summer savory, chopped; or ½ teaspoon dried and finely crushed (essential for fava beans, but optional for the green or pole beans)
>
> Salt to taste

If using fava beans, shell them and discard the pods. If using green beans, snap off the stem ends. If using pole beans, remove strings and snap off the ends; cut into 1-inch pieces.

Boil the fava beans in the 2 cups of water for about 25 minutes, or until done to your liking. Steam or boil the green beans or the pole beans. Drain and set aside. Combine the lamb or beef broth, butter, and seasonings in a saucepan and cook over low heat until the butter has melted. Add the beans to the pan, stir to combine, and heat through.

For a modern meal, serve as a side dish for a dinner of roast beef, potatoes au gratin, and cucumber salad.

Carrots & Parsnips ◊

Parsnips are an underused yet ever so flavorful winter vegetable. They pair well with their carrot cousins, and a handful of parsley adds extra vitamins. This recipe was developed in hearth cooking classes. It is an excellent recipe for fireplace cooking; see instructions below.

NOTE: Carrots take longer to cook than parsnips; therefore, boil the carrots for 3 or 4 minutes and then add the parsnips and finish cooking until both vegetables are soft, about 5 minutes more.

> 1 pound carrots
> 1 pound parsnips
> 2 tablespoons salted butter
> 3 tablespoons chopped parsley
> 1 teaspoon sugar
> Salt and freshly ground pepper

Peel the vegetables and cut into even sticks about 3 inches long by ¼ inch wide. In a medium saucepan or a pan suitable for fireplace cooking, add the vegetable sticks and about 1 cup water. See note above. For fireplace cooking, add enough water to cover the vegetables. Prepare a "burner" in the fireplace as described in "General Instructions for Fireplace Cooking" (pp. xiii–xv). Boil until done to your liking. Drain off any liquid that remains and add the butter and parsley. Season with sugar, salt, and pepper. Shake the pan to combine the ingredients. Add the chopped parsley, cover the pan, and heat the vegetables through.

For a modern meal, serve as a side dish with baked or grilled fish and baked potatoes. To cook potatoes in the fireplace, tightly wrap in aluminum foil and bake in the coals until they can be pierced with a fork.

Cauliflower or Savoy Cabbage
with Boiled Egg Yolk & Nutmeg

In this recipe, a sprinkling of mashed egg yolk gives color to the cauliflower and combines nicely with the nutmeg seasoning. Savoy cabbage can be prepared in the same way. The recipe in *De Verstandige Kock* says to cook the cauliflower or cabbage and "stew it with Mutton-broth, whole Pepper, Nutmeg, Salt, without forgetting the excellent Butter of Holland. A hardboiled egg yolk, which has been rubbed fine is sometimes placed underneath." Literally in the text: "underneath," but more likely on top as is still done today.

> 1 cauliflower, or 1 savoy cabbage
> 4 tablespoons salted butter
> 3 tablespoons lamb or beef broth (use water, if unavailable)
> 8 whole peppercorns
> ¼ teaspoon freshly grated nutmeg
> 1 or 2 hard-boiled egg yolks, mashed
> 2 tablespoons minced parsley, optional

If you are using cauliflower, remove any green leaves, break off the florets, and discard the core. Steam the florets until tender. If you are using savoy cabbage, pull off the leaves, discarding the outer, tougher ones as well as the core. Chop the tender leaves in 1-inch pieces and steam until done. Set aside.

In a large saucepan, melt the butter, then add the broth, peppercorns, and nutmeg. Allow to simmer on low heat for 10 minutes, then strain and return to the pan. Add the cauliflower or cabbage and heat through. To serve, place the cauliflower or cabbage in a bowl and sprinkle with the mashed egg yolk. A little minced parsley accentuates the color. *De Verstandige Kock* suggests serving the cauliflower in a deep bowl with a rim. The rim is rubbed with butter and sprinkled thickly with minced parsley.

For a modern meal, serve as a vegetable side dish with fried fresh sausage and crusty bread.

Coleslaw

The quality of butter, which depends on its freshness and the percent-age of butter-fat, greatly influences the outcome of most dishes. It is an ingredient frequently found in *De Verstandige Kock*. Some recipes include admonishments like "especially do not forget the butter," or "without forgetting the excellent butter of [the province] of Holland" (see previous recipe) which was considered the best.

In his *Borgerlijke Tafel* of 1633 (Bourgeois Table), Physician Stepha-nus Blankaarts proclaimed that "Butter is God's blessing to our coun-try." He said so no doubt not only for its healthful qualities but also for its importance as a trade good for the Dutch.

Butter was even used as a method of payment in New Netherland. When a community shepherd was hired in "Haarlem" (Harlem, Man-hattan) he received a cash stipend plus half a pound of butter for each cow in his flock. Butter rather than oil was used in the Netherlands and New Netherland. When Swedish botanist Pehr (Peter) Kalm visited the Dutch in the Albany area in the mid-eighteenth century, he described being served a dish unknown to him that consisted of the finely cut inner leaves of cabbage, mixed with a warm dressing. He adds that for this dish "butter is frequently used." The butter was mixed with vin-egar and kept warm in a pot by the fire. The dish was our present-day coleslaw; the word coleslaw comes from the Dutch "*kool*," Dutch for cabbage and "*sla*," Dutch for slaw or salad.

> 4 tablespoons salted butter
> ½ cup wine vinegar
> Salt and freshly ground pepper
> 2 cups green cabbage, cut into thin strips
> 2 cups red cabbage, cut into thin strips

In a saucepan, melt the butter, stir in the vinegar, salt, and pepper, and heat through. Pour the dressing on the cabbage and toss to combine. Make sure the cabbage is at room temperature when dressed and be sure to keep the coleslaw at room temperature, or the dressing will con-geal. Allow to stand at least 1 hour before serving.

For a modern meal, serve as a side dish. It is particularly good, of course, with fish and French fries.

Cooked Salads

These salads are very practical for buffets or large dinner parties. All kinds of cooked vegetables can be served at room temperature with a dressing of olive oil (or melted butter), vinegar, salt, and pepper. *De Verstandige Kock* suggests, among others, small head lettuces, Belgian endive, green or pole beans, onions or leeks, red and green cabbage cut fine, and beets.

For a red cabbage salad or a beet salad, the book suggests adding dried currants and a little sugar to the dressing. Allow the salad to stand at room temperature 1 hour before serving.

For a modern meal, cooked vegetable salads make excellent additions to almost any dinner.

Fried Green Leaves

This recipe illustrates the sometimes whimsical nature of *De Verstandige Kock*. It is a fun dish to prepare with children, who love to beat the eggs and fit the leaves together. Borage, with its light cucumber flavor, is delightful here, and if you happen to grow it, you can let the children pick the leaves. (Please note: Health authorities say that borage leaves should be used in moderation, as they may affect the stomach or digestion.) Otherwise, use romaine lettuce leaves. The original recipe reads: "To fry green leaves. Take young leaves of bugloss, borage, or clary and break off the stem, take out the ribs from the middle of the leaf without breaking that [the leaf], wash the leaves and put them down to drain dry, place beaten eggs in a flat dish and dip the leaves in it and fit two leaves together, the backs on the outside, then fry in butter and grate sugar over them." In the seventeenth century these fried leaves would have been served as a side dish.

Borage leaves, or the smaller inner leaves of romaine lettuce, washed and patted dry

2 eggs

4 tablespoons salted butter

Granulated sugar

With a sharp knife trim the thick ribs in the middle of the leaves, making sure the leaves still hold together. Beat the eggs in a flat dish with 1 tablespoon of water. Dip the inside of two leaves in the egg mixture, then fit the leaves together, the backs facing out. Dip both sides of the package in the egg mixture and shake off excess. Place a frying pan over moderately high heat and melt the butter. Quickly fry the leaves on both sides until lightly browned. Remove from the pan to serving plates and sprinkle lightly with sugar.

For a modern meal, try these as a side dish for pork or ham. Kids love them as a special snack.

Lovage or Sorrel Soup

Lovage and sorrel appear in the 1683 edition of *De Verstandige Kock* in a variety of recipes. They are herbs that have gone out of fashion (but are still available at some nurseries). They both have many good uses, such as adding lovage to stews or meat-based sauces (lovage is called the "meat herb" in Dutch); or adding the tart sorrel leaves to salads. (A recent red-veined variety makes a very attractive salad addition.) They are both great in soup as you will find when you make the following recipe.

1 tablespoon olive oil

1 medium onion, or 3 scallions, chopped

1 medium baking potato, peeled and cut into chunks

4 cups beef broth for Lovage Soup OR

4 cups chicken broth for Sorrel Soup

6–8 sprigs parsley

4–6 ounces lovage, 2 large handfuls OR

4 ounces sorrel, 2 large handfuls

Salt and freshly ground pepper to taste

¼ cup heavy cream

In a heavy saucepan, heat the olive oil. Add the chopped onion or scallions and fry just a few minutes to soften, add the potato chunks and broth. Bring to a boil and cook until the potato is done, about 12 minutes. In a blender combine parsley and either lovage or sorrel, then pour in the hot potato-broth mixture and blend until a nicely green soup is obtained. Taste and season with salt and pepper. Add the cream and blend for 10 more seconds. Pour back into the pan and reheat, or chill. Both soups can be served hot or cold.

For a modern meal, serve as a first course or a lunch dish.

Mushroom Fricassee

Anne Stevenson van Cortlandt's (1774–1821) original recipe calls for claret or dry red wine; I prefer using sherry. Use your own judgment.

The recipe reads: "Stew them and pour away the liquor. Fry them with a little butter and Onions. Shred small some sweet marjoram and Thyme stript from the stalk. Season it—with salt and pepper—Make a Sauce of Eggs beat in with the Juice of Orange, Claret, the Gravy of a Leg of Mutton & Nutmegg—Shake them well—give them a few tosses in the Pan. Put them in a dish rubbed with shallots, garnished with Lemon or Orange."

> 1½ pounds mushrooms, cleaned and sliced
>
> 2 tablespoons salted butter
>
> 1 medium onion, finely chopped
>
> ¾ teaspoon EACH minced fresh marjoram and thyme leaves, or a scant ¼ teaspoon EACH dried
>
> Salt and freshly ground black pepper
>
> 3 eggs
>
> 3 tablespoons good red wine or dry sherry
>
> Juice of 1 orange
>
> ¼ teaspoon freshly grated nutmeg
>
> 2 or 3 tablespoons juice from a beef or lamb roast, if available

Place the mushrooms in a large skillet set over low heat, and allow them to warm until they give off all their juices. Drain, discarding the juices. Wash and dry the skillet, and set over moderate heat. Add the butter and allow to color lightly, then add the mushrooms, onion, marjoram, and thyme. Season with salt and pepper and fry for a few minutes until the onions are translucent. In a small bowl, beat together the eggs, wine or sherry, orange juice, nutmeg, and meat juice (if available). Pour the egg mixture over the mushrooms and cook over *low* heat, allowing the eggs to set somewhat before stirring. The mixture will thicken and look more or less like scrambled eggs. The original recipe suggests serving this preparation in a dish rubbed with shallots with a garnish of lemon or orange wedges.

For a modern meal, serve as a handsome first course or a luncheon dish. A crusty roll and a small glass of the same wine or sherry used in the dish make excellent accompaniments.

Mushroom Quiche without a Crust

The recipe was adapted from *Traktaet van de Kampernoeljes, Genaamd Duivelsbrood* (Treatise of Mushrooms, Named "Devil's Bread") (1668) by Franciscus van Sterbeeck. You'll find it is remarkably easy to make.

> 10 ounces white mushrooms, wiped clean
> 1 clove garlic, minced, or 2 tablespoons finely chopped chives
> ¼ teaspoon EACH freshly ground pepper, salt, and dried marjoram
> 2 tablespoons minced parsley
> 1 cup grated aged Gouda cheese
> 3 eggs, beaten with ⅓ cup of milk

Preheat the oven to 375°F. Break off mushroom stems and chop. In a large bowl, combine stems, garlic or chives, seasoning, cheese, and eggs. Place mushroom caps, opening up, in a 9-inch pie plate in an even layer and pour the egg mixture over the caps. Bake for 10 minutes at

375°F and reduce the heat to 325°F and bake for 30 minutes until set. Cut into wedges and serve.

For a modern meal: serve with a large mixed salad and crusty rolls or whole grain bread to make a light but delicious lunch. This might also be added as a vegetarian option to Thanksgiving dinner.

Salad of Mixed Greens

This recipe shows once again that what we think of as modern dishes have been around for a long time. Today's salads of mesclun and edible flowers were served more than three hundred years ago! The original recipe in *De Verstandige Kock* needs no adaptation.

"To prepare raw salad: Take head, leaf lettuce, curly lettuce, lamb's lettuce (lamb's ear), also the shoots of the dandelions or wild chicory, also the shoots of chicory roots (Belgian endive), or red and white (green) cabbage, or cucumbers, whatever one has on hand that is best or that is in season and well cleaned is eaten with a good oil of olives, vinegar, and salt. On some [vegetables] additional herbs are used according to everyone's desire, but the usual are cress, catnip, purslane, burnet, rocket, tarragon, buttercup, one may also add the flowers of Bugloss, borage, rose and calendula. This salad is also eaten with melted butter and vinegar gently heated together instead of oil and vinegar, according to everyone's desire." (If the salad is served with a melted-butter dressing, be sure that the greens are at room temperature; otherwise the butter will congeal and the salad will look unappetizing.)

For a modern meal, serve as a first course.

Sliced Turnips, Braised with Butter & Sugar

Next to lima beans and broccoli, turnips are one of the most maligned vegetables. Yet you will be surprised how a bit of butter and sugar will turn this vegetable into a side dish that even the kids will like. Here is the original recipe from *De Verstandige Kock*: "Take turnips which have been cut into strips, then place them in a flat [shallow, earthenware] pot with half a small bowl of water. Let them stew a bit with butter and often shake them."

1 pound turnips, thinly peeled and sliced and cut into
¼-inch strips

3 tablespoons salted butter

1 teaspoon sugar

Salt and freshly ground pepper

Boil the turnips in 2 cups water until they can be easily pierced with a fork (about 5–8 minutes). Drain and set aside. In the same pan, melt the butter and stir in the sugar. Add the turnip strips and shake the pan to combine. Season with salt and pepper.

For a modern meal, serve as a vegetable side dish with a ham slice, sweet potato oven fries, and a salad.

Main Course Dishes

THE RECIPES IN THIS CHAPTER begin with a cheese *taert* suitable as either a main course or an hors d'oeuvre, and also encompass meats, poultry, and seafood. Most are modern versions of recipes from the 1683 edition of *De Verstandige Kock*. As with the vegetable recipes, some of these recipes are simple, while others are more complex, surprising us by using familiar foods in unusual ways. The dishes indicated with a small flame are particularly suitable for fireplace cooking.

Cheese

Cheese *Taert*

The following recipe makes a flavorful savory cheese *taert* that can be a meal in itself for 6 or more, or can be served in small wedges as an hors d'oeuvre. The almond decoration is my own addition. The original recipe reads: "Take little fresh Cream chees and Egg yolks with Wheat flour and Butter and make a dough[-like filling] from it, place it in your crust. It is good."

NOTE: Do not make this *taert* unless you have young, soft Gouda cheese (best purchased at a cheese shop); otherwise the filling will be too dry.

For the crust:

2 cups all-purpose flour

11 tablespoons (1 stick plus 3 tablespoons) cold, salted butter, cut into pats (do not use margarine)

2 egg yolks, lightly beaten with a fork

1 teaspoon salt

For the filling:

1 pound young Gouda (see note above)

¼ cup whole wheat flour

4 eggs

2 tablespoons salted butter, melted and cooled

About 41 whole natural unblanched almonds

Preheat the oven to 375°F. Lightly butter a 9-inch springform pan. In the work bowl of a food processor fitted with the metal blade, combine the flour, butter, egg yolks, and salt. Process just until a cohesive dough forms. Press the dough on the bottom and 1¼ inches up the sides of the prepared pan. Run your thumb around the rim to even it.

Cut the cheese in small pieces and combine with the flour in the work bowl of a food processor fitted with the metal blade. Pulse-process until the cheese is finely chopped. Alternatively, grate the cheese on the shredding plate of a box grater, then toss with the flour until the shreds are separated. Using an electric mixer, whip the eggs until frothy, then add the grated cheese, flour, and melted butter and beat until smooth. Spoon the filling into the crust. Carefully smooth the top and decorate with a circle of almonds along the rim. Neatly place three almonds in the center. Bake for 45 to 50 minutes, or until the filling is firm and light gold. Do not overbake; it will make the filling rubbery. Serve warm or at room temperature. The cheese *taert* can be made a few hours ahead.

For a modern meal, pair the *taert* with a salad for an excellent lunch or light dinner. When the *taert* is cut into thirty-eight ¾-inch wedges (the width of an almond), it makes a surprisingly easy-to-serve accompaniment to drinks.

Meats

Brabant *Hutspot* with Ginger

See my essay, "Dutch Foodways: An American Connection."

This stew from the southern province of Brabant is added because it is particularly suitable for fireplace cooking and is an example of the one-pot dishes discussed in my essay. It makes a warming winter family dinner. The ginger seasons the stew without making it spicy. The original in *De Verstandige Kock* reads: "[T]ake beef, cook it until almost done then add peeled ginger cut into slices with mace, continue to stew until done, take some of the broth, cook it with chopped parsley and butter, pour it over [the stew]."

> 6 tablespoons salted butter or oil, or 3 tablespoons each
> 1½ pounds stew beef, cubed
> 2- to 3-inch piece of ginger (about ½ cup), peeled and cut crosswise into very thin slices
> 2 teaspoons sugar
> ¼ teaspoon ground mace
> 1 teaspoon salt, or to taste
> 1 cup water
> ½ cup chopped parsley
> 2 tablespoons salted butter for the gravy

Heat the butter and/or oil in a heavy pan and brown the meat cubes on all sides. Add the ginger, sugar, mace, and salt just before you finish browning the meat. Stir well, then add the water. Bring the stew to a boil, then reduce the heat to low and cover the pan. For fireplace cooking, the recipe can be prepared on the stove up to this point. Then prepare a "burner" in the fireplace as described in "General Instructions for Fireplace Cooking" (pp. xiii–xv). Place the pot on a trivet over the coals. Simmer for about an hour or until the meat is tender. Check occasionally, adding a little water if the meat looks dry. When done, pour off or ladle the gravy into a small pan. Add the chopped parsley. Cut the two tablespoons butter into pats and stir them one by one into the gravy. Pour back into the pan with the meat and combine.

For a modern meal, serve with boiled or baked sweet potatoes and green beans, peas, or snow peas.

Calf's Ears

No, the recipe is not for actual ears of calves but for small bread slices topped with a well-seasoned chopped veal mixture. It makes an elegant dish despite its name. The original recipe reads: "[T]ake chopped veal which is done, add to it nutmeg, mace, sugar, and 2 or 3 egg yolks, stir together, then take sliced white-bread and place the above on the bread and fry it like this together in a pan in the butter."

> 2 cups finely chopped cooked veal or beef
> or
> ¾ pound veal stew meat, cubed
> ¼ cup white wine or water, if needed
> ¼ teaspoon freshly grated nutmeg
> Scant ¼ teaspoon ground mace
> 1 teaspoon sugar
> 3 egg yolks
> 8 slices, ½ inch thick, cut from firm, white, round dinner rolls, about 2½ inches in diameter
> About 3 tablespoons salted butter for frying
> Chopped parsley or thyme sprigs for garnish

If you are cooking the meat from scratch, heat a tablespoon of oil in a heavy frying pan and brown the cubed veal on all sides over high heat. Lightly season with salt. Add white wine or water to the pan, cover, and reduce the heat to low. Check after 10 minutes and add more liquid if necessary. Braise the meat for 45 minutes, or until tender. Finely chop the meat, making about 2 cups.

In a medium bowl, combine the cooked chopped meat, nutmeg, mace, sugar, and egg yolks. Spread about ¼ cup of the mixture on each roll slice, to cover it thickly. Heat the butter until sizzling in a frying pan large enough to hold 4 slices in one layer. Brown the bread side, then carefully turn with the aid of 2 spoons and cook the top. Remove to a plate, keep warm, and proceed with the next batch in the same manner. Serve warm, decorated with chopped parsley or thyme sprigs.

For a modern meal, serve for lunch accompanied by a salad, as a first course, or as a substantial plated hors d'oeuvre.

Fresh Ham Roasted with Cloves

There are several seventeenth-century still lifes with a roasted ham stuck with cloves, so we know that that was the way the meat was prepared even 400 years ago, at a time when West India Company ships brought large quantities of the spice from Asia.

> 1 fresh ham, 16 to 20 pounds
> Salt
> Whole cloves

Preheat the oven to 350°F. Rinse the ham and pat dry. Rub all over with salt. Using a metal skewer, puncture the skin at 1½-inch intervals and insert a clove in each hole. Place the ham skin side up in a roasting pan large enough to hold it comfortably. Roast for 25 minutes per pound, but check 1 hour before the allotted time is up. Use an instant-read thermometer to check the internal temperature; it will read 170°F when the meat is done. (Old meat thermometers indicate that pork is done at 190°F, but this is too much.) Cover the roast with foil and let rest at least 30 minutes before carving.

For a modern meal, carve and serve with warm, freshly made applesauce flavored with cinnamon, braised fava or green beans (p. 24), and potatoes.

Lemon Heart

This is a perfect dish for Valentine's Day! The recipe says: " . . . to shape it in the form of a large Meatball or in the form of a Heart." Preserved lemons are available in some Middle Eastern markets.

> 1 pound ground veal
>
> 1 egg yolk
>
> ¼ cup plain dry bread crumbs
>
> 1 teaspoon salt
>
> Freshly ground pepper and freshly grated nutmeg to taste
>
> Grated zest of 1 small lemon
>
> 6 tablespoons salted butter, divided
>
> Juice of 1 lemon
>
> Peel of 1 salted lemon, cooked in water to cover for 10 minutes, drained, and chopped, optional

In a large bowl, combine the veal, yolk, bread crumbs, salt, pepper, nutmeg, and lemon zest. On a cutting board, form into a flat heart shape. In a deep frying pan, lightly brown 4 tablespoons butter and brown the heart on both sides. Add between ½ and ¾ cup water, cover the pan, and gently simmer until the heart is cooked through, 20 to 30 minutes depending on thickness. Add the remaining 2 tablespoons butter, the lemon juice, and optional salted lemon. Cook gently for a few minutes more and serve.

For a modern meal, serve with mashed potatoes and a mixture of broccoli and cauliflower. Happy Valentine's Day (or any other day you feel like serving someone a heart-shaped dish . . .)!

Pea Soup

It is easy to see that pea soup made the Dutch way—in this case my mother's way—is a direct descendant of one-pot hearth meals. Start with 1 or 2 pig's feet for a good broth, add peas and what winter vegetables are available, and cook until thoroughly done for a soup with layers of flavor. The dried whole peas of the seventeenth century required hours of cooking to get soft, rather than the 20 to 30 minutes that today's split peas need. And seventeenth-century cooks never discarded the fat that floats to the top of the soup as we do today. In those days, fat was valued.

>   Two pig's feet, thoroughly cleaned, or 1 large ham bone with some meat on it, or 3 pounds beef soup bones plus a beef marrow bone
>   1 gallon cold water
>   1½ pounds loin end pork chops
>   2 pounds green split peas, rinsed and picked over to remove little stones or other foreign matter
>   4 large carrots, peeled and chopped
>   2 large leeks, including pale, tender portions of green tops, carefully washed, and cut into thin rounds
>   2 onions, peeled and chopped
>   3 large stalks of celery and at least 3 tablespoons of celery leaves, chopped
>   Salt and freshly ground pepper to taste
>   1 pound smoked sausage (such as kielbasa or smoked turkey sausage)
>   1 large handful fresh parsley, washed and chopped

Place the pig's feet, ham bone, or soup and marrow bones in a large soup pot and bring to a boil in *cold* water. Skim the surface carefully to remove the foam and other impurities. Simmer for 2 hours. Add the pork chops. Bring to a boil again and skim. Simmer for another hour. Remove the pan from the heat and cool to room temperature. Refrigerate overnight.

The next day take off and discard any hardened fat. Cut all meat off the bones and set aside; discard the bones. Strain the broth through a sieve, then pour back into the pan. Add the split peas to the broth and simmer gently for about 30 minutes or until they are soft. Add the vegetables and cook for another 30 minutes, stirring occasionally; this soup tends to burn at the bottom of the pot. Add the whole smoked sausage and the reserved cut-up meat. Gently simmer for 10 to 15 minutes longer. Taste; season with salt and pepper. Remove the sausage, cut it into slices, and return it to the soup, together with the chopped parsley. Serves eight or more.

For a modern meal, serve this soup with some bread and butter and have a baked apple for dessert.

Rabbit

"It tastes just like chicken" is what people always say when trying to convince the wary to eat rabbit. It does not, or at least it should not! It is a meat that can stand on its own, especially when prepared as follows. The recipe says that after the rabbit has been cooked in water and then fried in butter to brown, ". . . a sauce of Butter and some Vinegar and Sugar . . ." is added, and concludes: "It tastes all right."

> 1 rabbit, whole or cut up, thawed if necessary
> 12 tablespoons (1½ sticks) salted butter, divided
> 2–3 tablespoons white wine vinegar
> 1–2 teaspoons sugar, or to taste

Simmer the rabbit in just enough salted water to cover the meat and cook until tender, about 20 to 30 minutes. Remove to a colander and cut into pieces, if necessary, reserving the broth for some other purpose. Heat 6 tablespoons butter in a frying pan large enough to hold the pieces in one layer and brown them on both sides. In the meantime, melt 2 tablespoons additional butter in a small saucepan and stir in 2 tablespoons vinegar and 1 teaspoon sugar. Remove the pan from the heat. Stir in the remaining 4 tablespoons butter, pat by pat, until the sauce is slightly thickened. Taste. The sauce should be sour/sweet. Add more vinegar or sugar if needed. Remove the browned rabbit to a serving platter and pour on the sauce.

For a modern meal, serve with boiled chestnuts (pp. 23–24), a cooked salad of braised red cabbage dressed with a vinaigrette with currants (see Cooked Salads), and crusty bread or mashed potatoes.

Veal Meatballs in Head Lettuce

Don't be put off by the idea of boiled meatballs. This next recipe makes a tasty and pretty dish. The boiling gives the meat an appealingly dense texture, and the seasoning of mace and nutmeg pairs well with the slightly sour butter sauce about which the original recipe says: " . . . add to the broth a little crushed Rusk and some Butter, some Gooseberries or unripe Grapes or Verjuice, according to everyone's liking." (Verjuice or *Verjus* is the juice of pressed unripe grapes or other fruit.)

> 1 pound ground veal or beef
>
> 1 teaspoon salt
>
> Scant ¼ teaspoon EACH of freshly ground pepper, freshly grated nutmeg, and ground mace
>
> Yolks of 4 hard-boiled eggs
>
> 4 small heads Boston lettuce, thoroughly washed
>
> 2 cups water
>
> ½ cup gooseberries or unripe grapes, or 2 tablespoons verjuice, or lemon juice
>
> ¼ cup plain, dry bread crumbs, plus more if needed
>
> 2–3 tablespoons salted butter, cut into pats

In a medium bowl, combine ground meat, salt, pepper, nutmeg, and mace and knead together. Divide the mixture into four portions and shape into balls around each egg yolk. Open up the lettuce heads and place a meatball in the middle. Fold the leaves around the ball and tie with kitchen twine. In a pan large enough to hold the meatballs snugly in one layer, bring the water to a boil. Add the wrapped meatballs; gently cook for 15 minutes on one side and then turn and cook for another 15 minutes, or until the meat is done. Remove the meatballs and keep warm. To the broth, add the gooseberries or unripe grapes, or the verjuice or lemon juice, and ¼ cup bread crumbs. Stir and cook for 10 minutes. Strain if you used gooseberries or grapes; taste and adjust seasonings. Stir in the pats of butter one at a time; if the sauce does not seem thick enough, add more bread crumbs. Allow to simmer for another 5 minutes. Place the meatballs in a serving dish, remove the strings, and spoon the sauce over and around them.

For a modern meal, serve with boiled or baked potatoes and cooked beets with their greens.

Veal Meatballs with Orange

This recipe from the handwritten collection of Anne Stevenson van Cortlandt (1774–1821) is called "forced meat balls" in its original text and calls for a half pound of pepper, which is no doubt an error. Her recipe reads: "2 lb of veal ½ lb salt pork a slice of bread dipped in warm water ½ teaspoonful cayene pepper ½ lb black pepper 2 teaspoonsful of salt ½ teaspoon ful of thyme ½ teaspoonful onions and celery or parsley of orange peal, cloves and alspice each a teaspoonful & one egg. Wett your hands with water when you roll them" (n.d.).

> 1 pound ground veal
>
> 4 ounces salt pork, rind removed and finely chopped, optional
>
> 2 slices whole wheat bread, briefly soaked in water and squeezed dry
>
> 1 egg
>
> 1 tablespoon EACH minced onion and celery
>
> Pinch EACH of dried thyme, ground cloves, and ground allspice
>
> Grated zest of 1 orange
>
> 1 teaspoon salt
>
> Freshly ground pepper
>
> Dash of cayenne pepper
>
> 2–3 tablespoons salted butter or oil for frying

Thoroughly combine all ingredients except the butter or oil. Shape into 2-inch balls. In a frying pan, heat the butter or oil and fry the meatballs until nicely browned. Add about ½ cup water and cover the pan. Simmer for 10 to 15 minutes. Recipe may be doubled or tripled.

For a modern meal, serve with boiled or mashed potatoes and red cabbage braised with apples, raisins, butter, and nutmeg. Smaller meatballs also make an excellent hot hors d'oeuvre.

Poultry

Savory Raised Pie with Quail

While the original recipe called for finches, we will use quail instead in this *pastey* (the Dutch word for savory raised pie). Buy quail that are partially boned, with only the leg bones remaining. Warn your guests to eat carefully. I used here a rich, slightly sweet short crust, but you can also use the crust recipe from the spiced chicken *pastey* (see next recipe). Note that the crust recipe must be prepared in two batches.

> For the crust:
> Butter for the springform pan
> 22 tablespoons (2¾ sticks) cold, salted butter, cut into pats
> 4 cups all-purpose flour
> ½ cup light brown sugar, packed
> 4 egg yolks, lightly beaten with a fork
> 2 teaspoons rose water, if available

Lightly butter a 9- or 9½-inch springform pan. In the work bowl of a food processor fitted with the metal blade, combine *half* of the butter, flour, sugar, egg yolks, and rose water. Process just until a cohesive dough forms. Press the dough on the bottom and 1¼ inches up the sides of the prepared pan. Run your thumb around the rim to even it. Make a second batch of dough, using the remaining half of the ingredients. Wrap in plastic wrap and refrigerate.

> For the filling:
> 4 partially boned quail, weighing 4 to 5 ounces each
> ½ cup currants
> ¼ cup pine nuts
> 1 tablespoon finely diced citron
> 1 teaspoon ground cinnamon

1 teaspoon salt

2 teaspoons sugar, divided

4 tablespoons salted butter, cut into pats

½ cup dry white wine

In a pan wide enough to hold the quail in one layer, poach the birds in water to barely cover, until just done, or until the juices run clear when the meat is pricked deeply with a fork, about 15 to 20 minutes. Drain. Arrange the quail in the crust in a spoke pattern. Sprinkle with the currants, pine nuts, citron, cinnamon, salt, and ½ teaspoon sugar. Top with pats of butter.

Preheat the oven to 350°F. Between two sheets of plastic wrap, roll the second dough portion into a rough 10-inch circle. Using, if possible, the bottom of another springform pan of the same size as a template, cut out a neat 9-to 9½-inch circle, ¼ to ½ inch thick. Reserve the scraps. Peel off the top layer of wrap and use the bottom layer to help you ease the crust onto the filled *pastey*, making sure that it covers the rim of the bottom crust all around. Using a paring knife, gently press the edge of the top crust at ¼-inch intervals to fuse the top crust to the sides of the pastry. Do not press so hard as to cut through the crust. Freeze the scraps for later use, or, if you wish, use them to make leaves and flowers to decorate the top crust. Moisten the bottom side of each decoration with a little water before placing on the crust. Cut three gashes in the top crust to let steam escape. Bake for about 45 minutes to 1 hour, or until nicely browned. In a saucepan, heat ½ cup dry white wine and the remaining 1½ teaspoons of sugar. At the last moment, just before serving, pour this sauce into the gashes of the pie. Cut into wedges, in such a way that each diner gets a quail.

For a modern meal, serve this rich pastry as a main course with a salad of mixed greens, cucumbers, and tomatoes.

Spiced Chicken *Pastey*

This recipe was created with the help of Dutch master baker Peter de Jong. Note that the crust recipe must be prepared in two batches.

For the crust:

6 cups all-purpose flour

28 tablespoons (3½ sticks) lightly salted butter, cut into pats

2 eggs

Lightly butter a 9- or 9½-inch springform pan, 2½ inches deep. In the bowl of a food processor fitted with the metal blade, combine *half* of the flour, butter, and egg. Process only until the dough forms a ball. Press out over the bottom and up to the top of the springform pan. Run your thumb around the rim to even it. Make a second batch of dough using the remaining half of the ingredients. Wrap in plastic and refrigerate.

For the filling:

5 boneless, skinless chicken breast halves

3 ripe pears, peeled, cored, and cut into large dice

20 pitted prunes

1 cup dried cherries

¼ cup minced citron

1 cup pine nuts

2 tablespoons ground ginger

1 tablespoon ground cinnamon

1 teaspoon EACH salt, ground cloves, and freshly grated nutmeg

6 tablespoons salted butter, cut into small pats

½ cup dry white wine, mixed with 1 teaspoon of sugar

Gently poach the chicken breasts in water to cover until barely done, about 15–20 minutes. Remove, cool somewhat, and cut into bite-sized pieces. Place one-third of the chicken pieces in the crust. Top with one third of the pears, prunes, cherries, citron, and pine nuts. In a small bowl, mix the ginger, cinnamon, salt, cloves, and nutmeg. Sprinkle one third of this mixture over the fruits, then top with one third of the butter pats. Repeat two more times, making three layers. Level the filling with the back of a spoon. Pour the wine mixture over the filling.

Preheat the oven to 350°F. Between two sheets of plastic wrap, roll out the second dough portion into a rough 10-inch circle. Using, if possible, the bottom of another springform pan of the same size as a template, cut out a neat circle, ½ inch wider than the pan and ¼ inch thick. Reserve the scraps. Peel off the top layer of wrap and use the bottom layer to help you ease the crust onto the filled *pastey*. Arrange the top crust in such a way that the edge bends up all around against the sides of the pie. Gently press the two crusts together with your thumb. Using a paring knife, cut out a zigzag pattern in the protruding rim.

Cut a circle in the middle so steam can escape. Freeze the scraps for later use, or, if you wish, use them to create leaves and flowers to decorate the top crust. Moisten the bottom side of each decoration with a little water before placing on the crust. Bake for about 1½ hours, or until nicely browned.

For a modern meal, start with a salad, serving the *pastey* by itself as an impressive main course, and finish with fruit.

Stew of Chicken, Lamb, & Meatballs with Spring Vegetables

See "Dutch Foodways: An American Connection."

This stew with three different kinds of meats is included here because it is particularly suitable for fireplace cooking and is an example of the one-pot dishes discussed in my essay.

The original recipe in *De Verstandige Kock* reads: "[T]ake a good hen which has been cleaned well, boil it with some pieces of mutton and a little salt. When it is half done add in a stewing pan some sausages or small meatballs, also a good handful of endive, salad greens, sorrel and celery also asparagus. Especially do not forget the butter."

> 3 pounds chicken, cut into serving pieces
> 1 pound boneless lamb stew meat, cut into ½-inch cubes
> 1½ teaspoons salt, divided
> About ½ pound ground veal or beef

Scant ¼ teaspoon EACH freshly grated nutmeg, ground
mace, and freshly ground pepper

4 tablespoons salted butter

1 cup finely cut escarole

1 cup thinly sliced sorrel, if available

1 cup thinly sliced celery with leaves

½ pound asparagus, cleaned, woody ends snapped off, and
cut into 1½-inch pieces

In a large pan, combine the chicken pieces and the lamb stew meat. Cover
(barely) with water, add 1 teaspoon salt, and bring to a boil. Carefully
skim off the foam. Reduce the heat and gently simmer until the lamb
is tender, 40 to 60 minutes. For fireplace cooking, prepare a "burner," as
described in "General Instructions for Fireplace Cooking" (pp. xiii–xv).
Place the pot on a trivet over the hot coals. In the meantime, thoroughly
combine the ground meat, nutmeg, mace, pepper, and remaining ½ teaspoon salt and form into 1½- to 2-inch meatballs, flattened.

On the stove or on another fireplace "burner," nicely brown the meatballs on both sides in the butter in a frying pan, then add them to the
chicken and lamb. When the chicken is done, ladle out about half of the
cooking broth and save for another use. Add the vegetables to the pan and
cook for about 5 minutes, or until the asparagus and celery are tender.

For a modern meal, serve straight from the pan, accompanied by
lots of crusty bread and butter.

Turkey with a Parsley & Lemon Sauce

Turkey is eaten more and more year-round. For the following recipe,
stay away from accompaniments that remind us of the Thanksgiving meal and surround the bird with spring and summer vegetables.
"Crammed full of parsley," as the original recipe in *De Verstandige
Kock* reads, the bird is boiled and the herb is used for a flavorful sauce
that will go well with any of the new varieties of potato (small red bliss,
fingerling, baby Yukon, or creamer potatoes). If boiling a turkey seems
too outlandish to you, simply roast the parsley-filled bird and serve it
with the sauce as indicated below.

    1 young turkey, weighing 8 to 10 pounds, rinsed inside
and out

    Large bunch parsley, carefully washed

    2 teaspoons salt

    8 tablespoons (1 stick) lightly salted butter

    4 tablespoons lemon juice

Stuff the turkey with the parsley. Place it in a pan large enough to hold it comfortably and add water to cover. Add salt and bring to a boil. Skim the surface carefully to remove the foam and other impurities.

Allowing approximately 20 minutes per pound, gently simmer the turkey until the juices run clear when the meat is pricked deeply with a fork; do not cook until the meat falls off the bone. Remove from the pot and place on a carving board; cover and let rest for 15 minutes.

In the meantime, in a saucepan melt the butter and add the lemon juice. Take the parsley out of the cavity and cut very fine. Stir into the butter sauce together with about ½ cup of the broth, taste, and adjust the seasonings with salt and pepper. (If you roast the bird, you might want to add some of the pan juices to the sauce.) Pour all but a few spoonfuls of the sauce into a large deep platter. Carve the turkey and arrange the slices on top of the sauce. Drizzle the reserved sauce over the top and serve immediately.

For a modern meal, serve with potatoes, wild rice or quinoa, and an assortment of spring and summer vegetables such as asparagus, small carrots, tiny artichokes, peas, and snow peas. Ice cream, fruit, and cookies for dessert will make this a very festive meal that is easy to prepare.

Fish & Seafood

A Good Dish of Crab

The Dungeness crab used in this dish is a cousin to the variety that the Dutch call the *Noordzee krab*, the common crab of western and northern Europe. The Dungeness crab is somewhat smaller but has very fine flavor.

Use 1 crab per person. Boil it yourself, or ask your fishmonger to do so. Unless you are very experienced, allow ample time (at least

30 minutes) to take out the meat of the shells. The recipe says to " . . . remove all the dirt from the Crab, add to it Parsley cut fine, Pepper, Mace, Nutmeg, and Butter. Stir it together until it is done."

> 1 teaspoon plus 4 tablespoons salted butter, divided
> 4 tablespoons minced parsley, divided
> Yolk of 1 hard-boiled egg, mashed
> 1 cooked Dungeness crab
> ¼ teaspoon freshly grated nutmeg
> ½ teaspoon ground mace
> Juice of ½ lemon

Have ready a deep plate with a wide rim; an old-fashioned soup plate will work nicely. Rub the rim with 1 teaspoon of butter and sprinkle with half of the minced parsley and all of the hard-boiled egg yolk. Set aside. Pull off the large top shell of the crab. Crack the remaining shell and legs. Scoop out the brown liver portion and reserve. (Some people mix the liver with a bit of mayonnaise and use it as a dipping sauce, but that is not part of the original recipe.) Discard any dirt or veins. Using a nut-cracker and pick, remove the meat from the shell and cut into bite-sized pieces. In a saucepan, melt the remaining 4 tablespoons butter and stir in the remaining parsley and the seasonings. Cook for a few minutes, then add the crab meat. Heat through and stir in the lemon juice. Spoon into the prepared plate and serve. If the top shell is pretty, wash it thoroughly and use it as a cover for the dish as you carry it to the table. Serves one.

For a modern meal, this is a perfect small meal for lovers! Begin with a salad of young greens, serve one crab per person with some good bread and lots of champagne, and finish with a big wedge of Strawberry *Taert* (pp. 85–86).

Baked Cod with Mace

Here is a recipe for fresh cod, which was gently stewed in a tin platter with "fire under it and above" (meaning the tin platter was covered with a lid upon which coals were heaped.) Nowadays we simply set the dish in the oven; see recipe below. Other firm-fleshed fish may also be prepared this way.

> 3 tablespoons salted butter, divided
> 1 pound fresh cod
> Coarsely crushed pepper
> ¼ to ½ teaspoon ground mace
> ½ cup plain dry bread crumbs
> 1 teaspoon salt
> Lemon wedges

Preheat the oven to 325°F. Lightly butter a shallow ovenproof dish. Add the fish and sprinkle with pepper, mace, bread crumbs, and salt. Place small pats of butter on top of the fish. Add just enough water to cover the bottom of the dish. Cover the dish with foil. Bake for about 20 minutes, or until done to your liking. Before serving, sprinkle with a few drops of lemon juice and serve with lemon wedges.

For a modern meal, serve with carrots and parsnips (p. 25) and wild rice or potatoes.

Baked Oysters

Oysters were abundantly available in New Netherland when the Dutch arrived and still can be found in the Hudson River (though not recommended for eating). Here is a simple way of baking them. Recipes for oyster "stew" appear in many of the handwritten manuscript cookbooks handed down for generations in families of descendants of the early Dutch settlers.

> Butter for the soufflé dish
> ¼ cup plain dry bread crumbs, either commercially prepared or made from slices of stale bread
> ¼ teaspoon ground mace
> ½ teaspoon black pepper
> 1 pint shucked oysters with their liquor

About 4 tablespoons salted butter in thin slices
Lemon wedges for garnish

Preheat the oven to 350°F. Generously butter a 1-quart soufflé dish or small, deep casserole. Mix together the bread crumbs, mace, and pepper. Spoon enough oysters into the dish to cover the bottom in one layer; cover with a thin layer of the bread crumb mixture and top with thin slices of butter. Repeat until the oysters are used. The top layer should be bread crumbs and butter. Bake for about 40 minutes, or until lightly browned and bubbly.

For a modern meal, serve with a wedge of lemon and a crusty roll, either as a first course for four people, or as a luncheon dish for two.

Pike in the French Manner

Pike is easily available, especially during the Jewish holidays, because it is a main ingredient of gefilte fish. This recipe, with its combination of pike fillets and bacon, is very satisfying, flavorful, and filling. Other firm-fleshed fish may be substituted. The original recipe says that after the fish is boiled, a sauce is made with browned bacon cooked with " . . . broth, Rhenish wine, Vinegar, Mace, Pepper, and Ginger . . . ;" see below.

2 tablespoons salted butter
4 strips thick sliced lightly smoked bacon ("slab bacon"),
or use 8 strips regular bacon, cut in half lengthwise and across into cubes
½ cup dry white wine
3 tablespoons white distilled vinegar, divided
¼ teaspoon ground mace
Freshly ground white pepper, to taste
2 slices fresh ginger, each the size of a quarter, peeled
2 cups boiling water
1 pound pike fillets

Place the butter in a medium saucepan, set over moderate heat, and cook until golden. Add the bacon and fry until browned. Add the wine,

1 tablespoon of the vinegar, and the mace, pepper, and ginger. Simmer for about 15 minutes, or until the sauce has cooked down and thickened slightly. In the meantime, heat the oven to 225°F. Pour the water and remaining 2 tablespoons vinegar into a wide pan. Bring to a bare simmer. Salt the fillets and poach them in this water until you can flake the fish with a fork. Remove fish to a serving dish with a tablespoon of the poaching liquid. Cover and keep warm in the oven. Slowly add half a cup of the poaching liquid to the sauce, which will then thicken slightly more. Heat through and spoon over the fish. Serve immediately.

For a modern meal, crusty white bread and butter, or rice, and steamed broccoli, or cooked carrots mixed with lots of chopped parsley, and a salad make good accompaniments.

Pike in the Spanish Manner

See remarks regarding pike in the previous recipe. This recipe is lighter than the French version and has a bright, intense lemon flavor. "Take a Lemon, cut it in slices, place them in a little pot with some Rhenish wine, Water, Butter, Ginger, Saffron and Cloves, let it stew together . . ."

> 1 lemon, scrubbed and thinly sliced
>
> 1 cup dry white wine
>
> 3 cups water, divided
>
> 4 tablespoons salted butter
>
> 2 slices fresh ginger, each the size of a quarter, peeled
>
> 3 whole cloves
>
> ¼ teaspoon saffron, soaked in 2 tablespoons hot water for 10 minutes
>
> 2 tablespoons white distilled vinegar
>
> Salt to taste
>
> 1 pound pike fillets

In a saucepan, combine the lemon slices, wine, 1 cup water, butter, ginger, cloves, and saffron water and simmer for 20 minutes. Bring to a boil in a shallow pan the remaining 2 cups water, vinegar, and salt.

Turn down the heat so that the liquid barely simmers, add the fillets, and gently poach until the fish can be flaked with a fork. Pour the butter-ginger sauce (strained if you prefer) into a serving dish and place the fish in it.

For a modern meal, accompany the fish with boiled red potatoes, asparagus, and a mixed salad.

Salmon in a Thickened Pepper Sauce

The following is an easy and tasty way of preparing salmon, always a popular fish today. It is prepared in a water and white wine vinegar sauce with bread crumbs, " . . . whole Pepper, half a Nutmeg, a little crushed Mace, no Salt."

> 1½ cups water
> ¼ cup white wine vinegar
> ½ teaspoon salt
> 20 peppercorns
> ½ teaspoon freshly grated nutmeg
> ¼ teaspoon ground mace
> 2 fresh salmon fillets, about 1 pound
> 4 tablespoons salted butter, cut into pats
> ½ cup plain dry bread crumbs

In a wide pan, combine water, vinegar, salt, peppercorns, nutmeg, and mace. Bring to a boil and simmer for 10 minutes. Place the salmon in the broth, cover the pan, and stew for 6 minutes, or until cooked through. Using a slotted spoon, remove the fish to a plate. Cover and keep warm. Stir the butter and bread crumbs into the broth, cook for 5 minutes on low heat, then return the fish to the sauce and heat through.

For a modern meal, serve with boiled Yukon gold potatoes, cucumber salad, and Braised Green Beans (pp. 24–25).

Breads, Pancakes, Waffles, & *Olie-koecken*

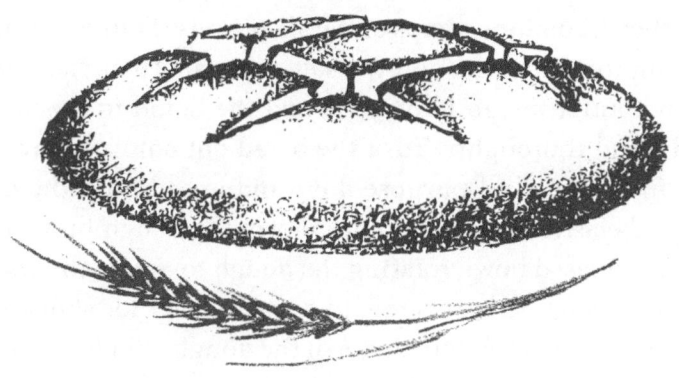

BAKING RECIPES were the trade secrets of the bakers. It was not until 1753 that the first ones were published in *Volmaakte Onderrigtinge ten Dienst der Koek-bakkers of hunne Leerlingen* (Perfect instructions for the pastry bakers or their students), but these did not include recipes for breads. Therefore, I include a recipe for a good, generic "brown" (whole wheat) bread that is easily baked in a Dutch oven in the fireplace, as well as one for crispy white dinner rolls. Also included are recipes from various sources for pancakes, waffles, and *olie-koecken* (forerunners of the doughnut), as well as one for a very traditional sweet bread. The dishes marked with a small flame symbol are particularly suitable for fireplace cooking.

Brown (Whole Wheat) Bread

The instructions that follow are for preparing the bread by hand. However, it can also be made very well in an electric mixer equipped with a dough hook. Follow manufacturer's instructions.

4 cups all-purpose flour
2 cups whole wheat flour
2 packages dry yeast
1½ teaspoons salt
2¼ cups milk
2 tablespoons honey
3 tablespoons salted butter
Cornmeal (for fireplace baking only)

In a large bowl, combine 3 cups of the all-purpose flour with the whole wheat flour, the dry yeast, and the salt. In a saucepan, heat the milk, honey, and butter to 120°F to 130°F; add the liquid to the flour mixture and blend thoroughly. Turn the bread out onto a floured board. Add the final cup of all-purpose flour and knead until the dough is smooth and elastic, 8 to 10 minutes. Form the dough into a ball and place it in a greased bowl, rotating the dough to grease the entire surface. Let the dough rise, covered, in a warm place for about an hour, or until doubled in bulk. Punch down the dough, divide it in half, and shape into two balls. Let the loaves rise again until doubled, about 45 minutes.

In the meantime, preheat the oven to 350°F. Place the round loaves on a baking sheet and bake for about 20 minutes. The loaves are done when they are nicely browned and the bottom of the loaf sounds hollow when lightly tapped, or an instant-read thermometer reads 200°F.

To bake the bread in the fireplace instead, prepare a "burner" in the fireplace, as described in "General Instructions for Fireplace Cooking" (pp. xiii–xv), about 10 minutes before the loaves are ready and place the Dutch oven on it (if necessary on a trivet) to heat through. Reshape the loaves into oblongs, so they will fit side by side in the Dutch oven. Sprinkle the bottom of the Dutch oven with cornmeal, place the loaves on top, and close the lid. Bread baking requires more heat on top than on the bottom, so put a thick layer of coals on top of the lid. Bake for about 20 minutes; see above. Very carefully remove the lid. If you are afraid of spilling the coals into the pot, brush them off first.

For a modern meal, serve with stew or soup, or use for sandwiches.

Olie-koecken

See "Dutch Foodways: An American Connection."

This deep-fried pastry was and still is the treat at fairs and carnivals. Nowadays, *oliebollen*, as they are called in modern Dutch, are served in most Dutch households on New Year's Eve and New Year's Day. The original 1683 recipe from *De Verstandige Kock* reads: "For 2 pounds of wheat-flour take 2 pounds long raisins, when they have been washed clean soak them in lukewarm water, a cup of the best apples, peel them and cut them in very small pieces without the cores, a quarter pound or one and a half peeled almonds, a *loot* [14 grams] cinnamon, a quarter loot white ginger, a few cloves this crushed together, half a small bowl of melted butter, a large spoon yeast, and not quite a pint of lukewarm sweet milk, because it must be a thick batter [so thick] that the batter is tough when spooned and then everything stirred together. Let it rise . . ."

When feeding a crowd, it is better to cut the *olie-koecken* in halves or quarters for serving than to make them in a smaller size. The almonds and apple pieces tend to distribute unevenly in miniature *olie-koecken*.

½ cup warm (100° to 110°F) water

3 packages dry yeast

Pinch sugar

8 tablespoons (1 stick) salted butter

1¾ cups raisins

4 cups all-purpose flour, divided

1 tablespoon ground cinnamon

½ teaspoon cloves

½ teaspoon ground ginger

¼ teaspoon salt

1½ cups milk

1 cup whole unblanched almonds

3 medium Granny Smith apples, peeled, cored and cut into small slivers

Oil for deep-frying

Confectioners' or granulated sugar, optional

Pour the warm water into a small bowl and sprinkle with the yeast and sugar. Let stand for a moment, then stir to dissolve the yeast. Set aside in a warm place. In the meantime, melt the butter and let cool. Place the raisins in a saucepan, cover with water, and boil for 1 minute. Let the raisins stand off the heat for 5 minutes, then drain. Pat dry with paper towels and mix with a tablespoon of flour. Place the rest of the flour in a large bowl and stir in the cinnamon, cloves, ginger, and salt. Make a well in the middle and pour in the yeast mixture. Stirring from the middle, slowly add the melted butter and the milk. Continue to stir until all the flour is incorporated and a very stiff batter forms. Add the raisins, almonds, and apples and combine thoroughly. Allow the batter to rise for about an hour, or until doubled in bulk, then stir down. Heat about 4 inches oil to 350°F in a large pot, or use a deep fryer. My mother taught me that *olie-koecken* should "swim in the oil." Dip a soup spoon in oil first then scoop out a heaping spoonful of batter. (Repeat this action for every scoop; this way the batter will not stick to the spoon.) The *olie-koecken* should be at least 2 inches in diameter. Holding the spoon just above the oil, carefully push the batter off with the aid of another spoon. Fry four or five at a time for about 5 minutes on each side, or until golden brown. You can check for doneness by cutting into one. Drain on paper towels. The original recipe does not tell us to sprinkle or roll them in sugar. They are very good plain, but if you prefer you can dust them with confectioners' sugar, or roll them in granulated sugar. Yield: about thirty.

For a modern meal, serve as a snack or as a breakfast treat. This is an excellent item for a bake sale.

Olicooks

See "Dutch Foodways: An American Connection."

Olicooks is the Anglicized word for the Dutch *olie-koecken*. I believe the cake-like *olicooks*, like the ones produced by this recipe (found repeatedly in Dutch American handwritten cookbooks), to be the direct forerunners of the American doughnut. In New Netherland, *olicooks* became the edible symbol of the Dutch in America and were served at most Dutch gatherings well into the twentieth century and still even today.

Here is a scaled-down version of a recipe from the handwritten cookbook of Anne Stevenson van Cortlandt (1774–1821). She might have obtained the recipe from the Van Rensselaer family in Albany, NY, because she calls it "*Olicooks* (Albany method)"; a similar recipe appears in the Van Rensselaer cookbook. "4 lb of flour, 1 lb butter 1 lb sugar 12 eggs a tea cup of yeast & [of] milk as much as you please say near or quite 3 pints."

> ¼ cup warm water (100° to 110°F)
> 3 packages of dry yeast
> Pinch sugar
> 8 tablespoons (1 stick) salted butter, softened
> ¾ cup sugar, plus more for coating
> 3 eggs
> 1 cup milk
> 4 cups all-purpose flour
> Oil for deep-frying

Pour the warm water into a small bowl and sprinkle with the yeast and the sugar. Let stand for a moment, then stir to dissolve the yeast. Set aside in a warm place. Cream together the butter and ¾ cup sugar. Beat in the eggs one at a time. Add the milk and yeast mixture. Slowly stir in the flour and combine thoroughly. Let the batter rise until fully doubled in bulk, about an hour. Heat 4 inches of oil to 350°F in a large pot, or use a deep fryer; like their Dutch predecessors, these *olicooks* must be able "to swim in the oil." Dip a soup spoon in oil first, then scoop out a heaping spoonful of batter. (Repeat this action for every scoop; this way the batter will not stick to the spoon.) Holding the spoon just above the oil, carefully push the batter off with the aid of another spoon. Fry 4 or 5 at a time, turning once, until golden. Check one *olicook* by cutting it in half to see if it is cooked through. Drain on paper towels. Roll in sugar to coat. Cool and serve. Yield: 25 to 30 *olicooks*.

For a modern meal, serve as a snack or for breakfast, or use as a bake sale item.

Pancakes, the Best

These are excellent examples of seventeenth-century pancakes. They are filling and stiff as a plank, so they could be eaten out of hand. The four spices give them mouth-filling flavor.

> 6 eggs
> Water
> 4 cups flour
> ¼ teaspoon EACH ground cloves, cinnamon, mace, and nutmeg
> Pinch of salt
> Butter for frying

Beat the eggs with a few tablespoons of water until light. Measure the liquid; you should have at least 2½ cups. If not, add more water. Combine flour, spices, and salt. Stir in the liquid to make a smooth batter. Use an electric mixer, if you wish. Heat 2 tablespoons butter in a frying pan. For a 5-inch pancake, spoon in ½ cup batter and level the top with the back of the spoon to make it ¼ to ½ inch thick. Fry on both sides until brown. Repeat with the rest of the batter. Yield: 8–10.

For a modern meal, top the pancakes with pats of butter and sprinkle with sugar and serve with a dried fruit compote of apricots or prunes for brunch or as dessert.

Pumpkin Cornmeal Pancakes

This recipe was re-created from Peter Kalm's travel accounts of the year 1749 (see References). He tells us that a thick pancake "was made by taking the mashed pumpkin and mixing it with corn-meal after which it was . . . fried." He found it "pleasing to my taste" (1987).

> 1 cup all-purpose flour
> 1 cup yellow cornmeal
> 1 cup confectioners' sugar
> ½ teaspoon ground ginger
> ½ teaspoon ground cinnamon

2 eggs

1 cup mashed, cooked pumpkin, fresh or canned

3 to 3½ cups milk

Salted butter for frying

In a large bowl, combine dry ingredients. In a medium bowl, beat the eggs lightly, then add the pumpkin. Beat into dry ingredients. Add milk slowly to make a smooth batter, the consistency of lightly beaten cream. Heat some butter in a crepe pan and pour in enough batter to make a 7-inch pancake. Do not make them too thin, or you will not be able to turn them. Fry until golden, about 3 minutes on each side. Yield: about 6.

For a modern meal, serve for breakfast or brunch. The pancakes are also an excellent dessert for a winter meal of stew or pea soup.

Rusks

The Dutch American rusks in Anne Stevenson van Cortlandt's (1774–1821) recipe are quite a bit sweeter than their seventeenth-century Dutch counterparts and were probably served with tea.

2 packages dry yeast

¼ cup warm water (100° to 110°F)

Pinch sugar

6 tablespoons salted butter

¼ cup sugar

1 egg

1¼ cups milk

3¼ cups flour

Sprinkle the yeast over the warm water, then sprinkle on the pinch of sugar. Let stand 2 minutes, then stir. Leave in a warm place until bubbly, about 5 minutes. Using an electric mixer, beat the butter and sugar until blended. Add the egg and milk and continue to beat for a few minutes until the mixture is light. Add the flour and yeast and beat until a dough forms. Form the dough into a ball and place in a greased bowl, rotating the dough to grease the entire surface. Let the dough rise, covered, in a warm place for about an hour, or until doubled in bulk. Punch the dough down and turn it out onto a floured surface. Pat it out into a layer 1½ inches thick and cut out into large rounds about 4 inches across (a tuna can opened on both sides makes an excellent improvised cutter). Combine the scraps, pat out, and cut more rounds. Place the rounds on greased baking sheets, cover with a towel, and allow to rise for 30 minutes, or until about doubled in bulk. In the meantime, preheat the oven to 300°F. Bake the rusks for 20 minutes, or until light brown. Remove from the oven and cool 10 minutes. Cut each rusk in half horizontally; place them, cut side up, on the baking sheets and bake, one sheet at a time, for another 10 to 12 minutes, or until light brown on top. Cool on racks.

For a modern meal, serve with butter and jam. They taste good any time.

Three-in-the-Pan

This is a modern recipe for a seventeenth-century treat. Three-in-the-pan pancakes are still favorites in the Netherlands today.

NOTE: The batter needs to stand for 1 hour.

> 2 packages dry yeast
> ¼ cup warm water (100° to 110°F)
> Pinch sugar
> 2 cups all-purpose flour
> Pinch salt
> 1½ cups milk, lukewarm
> 1 cup currants or raisins
> 2 medium Golden Delicious apples or other firm dry
> apples, peeled, cored, and chopped
> Salted butter for frying
> Confectioners' sugar

Sprinkle the yeast over the warm water, then sprinkle on the pinch of sugar. Let stand 2 minutes, then stir. Leave in a warm place until bubbly, about 5 minutes. Place the flour and salt in a deep bowl. Make a well in the middle and add the yeast mixture. Stirring from the middle, add the lukewarm milk a little at a time until the batter is smooth. Add the currants or raisins and chopped apples, and combine. Allow the batter to stand in a warm place for about an hour. Heat enough butter in a large frying pan to amply coat the bottom about ½ inch, and pour out batter to make three small (about 3-inch) pancakes. Fry on both sides until golden brown and serve hot, heavily dusted with confectioners' sugar and with just a small pat of butter in the middle. Yield: about 18 little pancakes.

For a modern meal, these pancakes make a delicious snack when the children come home from school, or an excellent dessert for a meal of hearty soup and bread.

Waffles

These waffles can, of course, be made in an electric waffle iron, but they are even more fun to make in the fireplace using a long-handled waffle iron, if you happen to own one. Just be sure to preheat the iron and to grease it with butter before each use, or the waffles will stick and you'll have a mess on your hands. These waffles are more bread-like than modern ones and not quite as light. In the seventeenth century they were served plain or with butter. The recipe in *De Verstandige Kock* reads: "For each *pond* of Wheat-flour take a *pint* of milk, a little tin bowl of melted Butter with 3 or 5 Eggs, a spoonful of Yeast well stirred together."

    1 package dry yeast
    ¼ cup warm water (100° to 110°F)
    Pinch sugar
    4 cups all-purpose flour
    4 tablespoons butter, melted and cooled
    2 cups milk
    2 eggs, beaten with a fork
    Butter for the waffle iron

Sprinkle the yeast over the warm water, then sprinkle in the sugar. Let stand 2 minutes, then stir. Leave in a warm place until bubbly, about 5 minutes. Place the flour in a large bowl, make a hollow in the middle, and add the yeast mixture and butter. Stir to combine. Slowly stir in the milk and then the eggs. Prepare a "burner" in the fireplace, as described in "General Instructions for Fireplace Cooking" (pp. xiii–xv). Place the iron on a trivet over the coals to preheat on both sides. Brush the iron with butter, ladle in a spoonful of batter, close the iron, and bake the waffle on both sides until golden. Follow the same preheating and baking procedures for an iron used on the stove, or for an electric iron.

For a modern meal, serve with butter and sugar for breakfast or with a glass of mulled wine (p. 93) on a cold winter day after an afternoon of ice-skating.

White Dinner Rolls

These rolls are best the same day that they are baked.

>   4 cups all-purpose flour
>   1 teaspoon salt
>   2 packages dry yeast
>   1½ cups water
>   4 tablespoons butter

Fit an electric mixer with a dough hook. Place 3 cups flour, salt, and yeast in the mixer bowl and beat on low speed for a few seconds to combine. In a saucepan heat water and butter to 120° to 130°F (the butter does not need to melt completely). Turn mixer on low speed and gradually pour the liquid into the flour. Then add the rest of the flour and continue mixing for about 5 minutes. By now, the dough will cling to the dough hook. Mix on low speed, or knead by hand for 7 to 10 minutes longer, or until the dough is smooth and elastic. Form the dough into a ball and place in a greased bowl, rotating the dough to grease the entire surface. Let the dough rise, covered, in a warm place for about 45 minutes, or until doubled in bulk. Punch the dough down. Remove to a very lightly floured surface and cut into 24 even pieces. Roll each piece into a neat ball and arrange on two greased baking sheets. Using scissors or a razor blade, cut or slash a cross in the top of each roll. Allow to rise again, covered by a kitchen towel, in a warm place until nearly doubled, about 20 to 30 minutes. In the meantime, preheat the oven to 425°F. Bake the rolls for 12 to 15 minutes, or until light brown on top. Cool on racks.

For a modern meal, these rolls are good any time of the day. Recipe can be cut in half, as necessary.

Zoete Koek (Spiced Sweet Bread)

Anne Stevenson van Cortland's (1774–1821) recipe uses honey and calls this sweet bread "Honey Cooke." The recipe closely resembles the modern version that follows made with dark brown sugar. The town of Deventer in the Eastern Netherlands has been known for this *zoete koek* or *Deventer koek* for centuries (a first mention of the product goes back to 1417).

> 1 cup dark brown sugar, packed
>
> 2 cups flour
>
> 1 teaspoon baking powder
>
> 1 teaspoon cinnamon
>
> ½ teaspoon freshly grated nutmeg
>
> ½ teaspoon ground cloves
>
> 1 cup milk

Preheat the oven to 350°F. In a large bowl, sift the dry ingredients together and stir to combine. Slowly add the milk and stir to make a dough without lumps. Spoon the dough into a greased 8 x 5 x 2½-inch loaf pan and bake for about one hour, or until a knife inserted comes out clean and the loaf is a deep brown. Cool and store. This is a dense loaf that keeps very well and improves in flavor and texture when stored in an airtight container for a few days.

For a modern meal: traditionally *zoete koek* is served for breakfast or as the accompaniment of a cup of coffee in mid-morning. It is the perfect sweet bread to bring to a church coffee hour. Serve the slices generously buttered!

Cookies

THE DUTCH WORD *koek* generally refers to a flat, not highly risen baked good and its diminutive *koekje* (or in seventeenth century Dutch, *koeck-jens* or *koecxkens*) is the root of the American word *cookie*. According to Charles T. Gehring, PhD, director of the New Netherland Research Center at the New York State Library in Albany, NY, it is quite possible that early Dutch settlers pronounced *koekje* as *koekie*, since the ie diminutive was a dialectal variation in the seventeenth century and is still a feature of western Dutch dialects.

Several cookie recipes are included in this chapter. All will make fun projects to do with children. The recipes marked with a small flame symbol are particularly suitable for fireplace cooking. Most of the recipes in this section are discussed in my essay, "Dutch Foodways: An American Connection."

Caraway Cookies

This recipe appears in several manuscript cookbooks of descendants of the early settlers of New Netherland. Today, Americans use caraway mostly in savory dishes such as braised sauerkraut; therefore, this sweet cookie is usually a (pleasant) surprise.

½ cup salted butter

1 cup sugar

2 eggs

1 tablespoon caraway seed, crushed with a rolling pin to release flavor

2 cups flour

Preheat the oven to 350°F. In an electric mixer outfitted with a flat beater, cream the butter with the sugar. Add the eggs one at a time and combine thoroughly. Add caraway and flour a little at a time and combine. Use two teaspoons to drop them on a buttered baking sheet about 1½ inches apart. Bake for about 15 minutes or until light brown. Cool on a rack and store in an airtight container. Yield: 4 dozen cookies.

Currant Cookies

The following recipe makes a satisfying crunchy and at the same time chewy cookie that is easy to make. It is another good project to do with children.

NOTE: Currants are often called "Zante currants;" they are small dried raisins and can be purchased in supermarkets.

1½ cups salted butter, softened

1 cup dark brown sugar

3 cups flour

1 cup currants (see note above)

Preheat the oven to 350°F. In an electric mixer outfitted with a flat beater, cream the butter and sugar; add the flour a little at a time and then stir in the currants. Pinch off pieces of dough and roll into 1-inch balls and place on a buttered baking sheet, spaced 2 inches apart.

Press down with a fork and make a crisscross pattern on top, or flatten with the bottom of a floured glass. Bake for 15–18 minutes. Transfer to racks and cool. Store in an airtight container. Yield: 3 dozen cookies.

Koecxkens

When I ate the results of my first experiment with the following recipe, I came to the conclusion that they tasted like exactly what they are supposed to be: "fried cookies." In English you would probably call them "fritters." They are very good. The recipe reads: "Take a Bread that is about 3 or 4 days old, grate it fine, then soak it in sweet Milk until it is thick and has absorbed the liquid, then take some Rosewater and Sugar and 6 or more Eggs according to how much Bread you have (some take also some Currants and Cinnamon with it) and then fry in Butter. Everyone [can make them] as big as he desires."

> 2 cups plain dry bread crumbs, made from 8–10 slices stale bread without crust
>
> 1¼ cup milk
>
> 3 eggs
>
> 2 teaspoons rose water (use 1 teaspoon vanilla extract instead, if you must)
>
> ¼ cup sugar
>
> ½ teaspoon ground cinnamon, optional
>
> ½ cup currants, optional (see note in previous recipe)
>
> Salted butter for frying

In a medium bowl, soak the bread crumbs in the milk until they have absorbed all the liquid, about 10 minutes. Beat the eggs with the rose water or vanilla extract and stir into the bread crumb mixture. Add the cinnamon and currants if used. Heat the butter in a frying pan, and fry the batter by the tablespoonful until brown on one side. Turn and brown the other side. Serve hot.

For a modern meal, serve these fritters at breakfast time, or as a substantial dessert after a meal of soup and bread.

Krakelingen

These pretzels are sweet rather than salty. They are meant to be hung on a rack, as was the custom in the seventeenth century. They are rather hard but good for dunking in today's cup of coffee or tea.

3 cups all-purpose flour

2¼ cup sugar

1 tablespoon ground cinnamon

1 teaspoon baking soda

4 tablespoons salted butter

2 eggs, beaten with a fork

Preheat the oven to 350°F. In a food processor fitted with the metal blade, combine flour, sugar, cinnamon, and soda and pulse to mix. Cut the butter into small pieces and add, together with the beaten eggs. Process until a dough ball forms. Divide into 8 pieces. Roll each into a rope 12 to 14 inches long and shape into a pretzel. Using a large spatula, place the pretzels on buttered baking sheets and bake for 15 minutes until brown and solid. Remove onto a rack to cool.

For a modern meal, use as a snack, perhaps with a cup of coffee or tea.

Letter Cookies

This recipe is included not only because it has historical significance—the forerunners of these cookies were made from bread dough and used to teach children their letters—but also because it is a fun project to do with older children age 8 and up. You might let them try to make the initial of their first name with a piece of string before they work with the dough, so they can discover how to go about forming the letter.

2 sticks salted butter

1 cup confectioners' sugar

2 egg yolks

3 cups all-purpose flour

Butter a baking sheet. In an electric mixer outfitted with a flat beater, cream the butter and sugar and add yolks, then the flour in 4 batches. Beat to make a smooth, non-sticky dough that clings to the beater.

METHOD 1: Divide the dough into 3 parts and work with 1 part at a time; refrigerate remaining dough. Roll out with a rolling pin about ½ inch thick and cut out with letter cookie cutters.

METHOD 2 is more fun to do with an older child: Divide the dough into 3 parts and work with one part at a time; refrigerate remaining dough. Roll each part into an even rope, about ½ inch in diameter, and 24 inches long, cut into 3 equal pieces. Roll each piece again and use to shape a letter. The dough is very easy to work with and very forgiving, just pat it in shape. Give the end(s) a small cut in the middle and then curl each side outwards to give the letter a finished look.

Preheat the oven to 325°F. Place the finished letters on the buttered baking sheet and bake for about 20–30 minutes until lightly browned. Cool on racks and store in airtight containers. Yield: 9–12 letters, depending on size.

New Year's Cakes

See "Dutch Foodways: An American Connection."

The addition of the orange zest makes these New Year's Cakes particularly flavorful. The recipe, from the handwritten cookbook of Maria Lott Lefferts (1786–1865) of Brooklyn, reads: "28 lb. of flour, 10 lb. of sugar, 5 lb. of butter, caraway seed and orange peal" (n.d.). Here is a much smaller version.

> 2 cups all-purpose flour
> ½ cup light brown sugar, packed
> ¼ teaspoon baking soda
> 8 tablespoons (1 stick) salted butter
> 1 egg, lightly beaten
> ¼ cup milk
> 1½ teaspoon caraway seed, crushed somewhat with a
> rolling pin to release flavor
> Grated zest of ½ orange

Sift all dry ingredients into a large bowl. If sifting the sugar is problematic, rub it between your hands to make sure no lumps remain. Combine the dry ingredients and butter in a food processor fitted with a metal blade, and pulse until the mixture looks like coarse meal. In a small bowl or measuring cup beat the egg and milk and pour into the flour-butter mixture, and add seeds and zest. Process until the dough comes together; wrap and cool for 1 hour. Preheat the oven to 300°F. On a floured board or counter, roll dough into 1-inch balls. Then flatten as thin as possible with the bottom of a floured glass. Carefully transfer to a buttered baking sheet and bake in batches for about 25–30 minutes, or until pale brown and crisp. Cool on racks and store in airtight container. Yield: at least 4 dozen, depending on size.

For a modern meal, these cookies are good anytime.

Speculaasbrokken (Spiced Cookies)

See "Dutch Foodways: An American Connection."

The word *brokken* means "pieces." In other words, this is meant to be a large cookie that is broken into pieces after baking. In the recipe that follows I shaped the dough into a square "log," cut it into ¼-inch thick slices to make small cookies, and topped each with an almond. In the Netherlands the spice mixture is factory made from secret formulas; here I combined seven different spices, creating my own mixture.

> 1 tablespoon milk
>
> ½ cup firmly packed dark brown sugar
>
> 6 tablespoons salted butter, cut into bits and softened
>
> 1 cup all-purpose flour
>
> ¼ teaspoon baking powder
>
> 1 tablespoon ground cinnamon
>
> ½ teaspoon ground mace
>
> ½ teaspoon ground aniseed
>
> ¼ teaspoon ground ginger
>
> ¼ teaspoon ground cardamom
>
> ¼ teaspoon freshly grated nutmeg
>
> ¼ teaspoon ground cloves
>
> ½ teaspoon salt
>
> 36 blanched whole almonds

Preheat the oven to 350°F. In a small bowl stir together the milk and the brown sugar. In a separate bowl combine the butter, the flour, the baking powder, the spices, the salt, and the brown sugar mixture. On a lightly floured work surface knead the dough until it is smooth. Form the dough into a 1¼-inch-square "log" and cut it into thirty-six ¼-inch slices. Arrange the slices 1 inch apart on a lightly buttered baking sheet and center an almond on each slice, pressing it in slightly. Bake the cookies in batches, one baking sheet at a time, in the middle of the oven for 10 to 12 minutes, or until they are golden. Transfer them to racks and let them cool. (The cookies will become firmer and crisper as they cool.) Store in an airtight container.

For a modern meal, serve these cookies anytime.

Tea *Cookjes*

See "Dutch Foodways: An American Connection."

Please note the half English–half Dutch spelling of the word *cookjes* in the title given this recipe by Maria Sanders van Rensselaer (1749–1830), wife of Philip van Rensselaer of Cherry Hill, Albany, NY. The original recipe from her handwritten book reads: "½ butt ¾ sugar 1 teacup water as much flour as it takes" (n.d.). With such simple ingredients, you might not imagine that these cookies would be any good, but they are! This is another good recipe to make with children. In a classroom setting, a toaster oven can be used for baking.

> 16 tablespoons (2 sticks) salted butter, softened
> 1½ cups sugar
> ¾ cup cold water
> 3½ cups all-purpose flour

Preheat the oven to 350°F. This recipe is easiest when made with an electric mixer. Cream the butter. Add the sugar a little at a time and continue creaming. Add the water alternately with the flour. Wrap the dough and refrigerate for 1 hour. Roll into ½-inch balls, which will make little dot-shaped cookies. Place ½ inch apart on buttered baking sheets and bake one sheet at a time for 14 to 16 minutes, or until lightly browned at the very edge and on the bottom. Makes at least 10 dozen.

For a modern meal, serve these hard, crisp, buttery cookies anytime. You cannot eat just one! Since the recipe makes a large quantity, they are very good for large gatherings, or for a church coffee hour.

Theerandjes

See "Dutch Foodways: An American Connection."

Theerandjes (literally "tea edges") is the Dutch word for these very chewy, clove-flavored honey bars, which are almost more a confection than a cookie and go well with a fragrant cup of tea. The original recipe comes from *Volmaakte Onderrigtinge ten Dienst der Kocek-bakkers of hunne Leerlingen* (Perfect Instructions for the Pastry Bakers or Their Students). Published in 1753, this was the first Dutch book with recipes for baking. Until then bakers kept their recipes secret.

> Salted butter for greasing the pan
> 1¼ cups sugar
> ⅔ cup honey, plus ¼ cup for the glaze
> 3 cups all-purpose flour
> 1 teaspoon ground cloves
> 1 teaspoon baking soda
> Candied orange peel, diced, see recipe below
> 2 tablespoons finely diced citron

Preheat the oven to 325°F. Heavily butter a 9-inch-square baking pan. In a saucepan bring the sugar and honey to a boil. Remove from the heat and cool slightly. Stir in the flour, cloves, and baking soda. Stir until thoroughly combined. Spread or pat the (stiff) dough in the prepared pan. Stir the remaining ¼ cup of honey with a tablespoon of warm water and brush the top of the dough with this mixture. Top sparingly with candied orange peel (about ½ cup) and the 2 tablespoons citron; their flavors are strong and you do not want to overwhelm the taste of the dough. Bake for about 30 to 35 minutes, or until a toothpick inserted in the center comes out clean. Cut while still warm into thumb-length strips, about ½- to ¾-inch wide and 3 inches long. Cool and store in an airtight container. These *Theerandjes* are highly flavorful and delightfully chewy. VERY IMPORTANT: Do NOT overbake as the strips will become hard. If this has happened, place them in an airtight container with several slices of fresh bread. This method will soften them. Another way to soften an individual piece is to place it in the microwave for 10 seconds and it will be soft enough to eat.

For a modern meal, serve with a cup of tea.

Candied Orange Peel

3 oranges
Water
Sugar

Scrub 3 navel oranges and peel off the skin as you would for eating. Place the peels in a saucepan and cover with water. Bring to a boil and simmer slowly for 10 minutes. Drain and repeat the process two more times. Drain the peels and with a knife remove any loose white pith. Cut the peel into ¼-inch strips. Measure, and for each cup of peel use a syrup of ½ cup sugar and ¼ cup water. Bring the syrup to a boil and add the peel. Simmer gently until the peel absorbs all of the syrup and is transparent. Use a candy thermometer and make sure the syrup does not reach more than 218°F, or it will start to brown and caramelize. When the peel is done, remove with a slotted spoon to a rack set on a baking sheet. Let the peel drain for 1 hour. In the meantime, process a cup of sugar in the blender to pulverize it. Roll the peel into the prepared sugar and then return it to the rack and let dry overnight. This orange peel can be used in the above recipe.

For a modern meal, serve this candied peel with some chocolates as a very nice "sweetmeat," perhaps with a glass of Raspberry Brandy (pp. 92–93), at the end of a meal.

Wafers 🔥

See "Dutch Foodways: An American Connection."

Wafers are thin round cookies made in a wafer iron over the fire or on the stove top. Lately Dutch *stroopwafels* or "syrup wafers" have become popular in the United States; they are used as "coffee toppers" (the hot coffee softens the syrup between the 2 wafers and makes them even more delicious.)

    2 cups flour
    ½ cup sugar
    1 teaspoon cinnamon
    ¾ teaspoon ground ginger
    1 egg, beaten light with a fork
    ½ cup dry white wine
    1 teaspoon rose water (omit if not available)
    4 tablespoons salted butter, melted and cooled
    Water for thinning the batter
    Butter for the wafer iron

In a large bowl, combine flour, sugar, and spices. Make a well in the middle, add the egg, and stir to combine. Add the wine, rose water, if used, and butter and combine thoroughly. Slowly add enough water (about ¼ cup), if necessary, to make a thick batter resembling pancake batter. Prepare a "burner" in the fireplace, as described in General Instructions for Fireplace Cooking (pp. xiii–xv). Place the iron on a trivet over the coals to preheat on both sides. A stovetop iron also needs to be preheated. Brush iron with butter on both sides, ladle in a spoon-ful; of batter, and close the iron. Bake on both sides. Scrape off any batter that might have oozed out. Open the iron and remove the wafer. Repeat until all of the batter is used.

For a modern meal, serve as you would cookies. Traditionally served with spiced wine, the wafers also would make a very nice accompaniment to the Peaches in Syrup (p. 82).

Desserts

MOST RECIPES in this section are modern versions of recipes from the 1683 edition of *De Verstandige Kock*, unless otherwise indicated.

Almond Tartlets

This recipe is based on one for a large almond *taert* but makes small individual pastries, ready to be served with tea or coffee. I used a so-called "cream crust" made with heavy cream instead of butter. Almond paste is a favorite ingredient in Dutch holiday baking and is often used in all kinds of baked goods.

> For the crust:
> 2¼ cups all-purpose flour
> ¾ cup sugar
> 1 egg yolk
> 1 cup heavy cream

In the work bowl of a food processor fitted with the metal blade, combine the flour and sugar. Run the machine a few seconds. Stir the egg yolk into the cream. With the machine running, pour into the flour mixture and process until the dough forms a ball. Wrap in plastic wrap and refrigerate.

For the filling:

2 cans, 8 ounces each, almond paste

2 teaspoons grated orange zest

2 large eggs, divided

Cut the almond paste into small pieces and place in the work bowl of a food processor fitted with a metal blade. Add the orange zest and one egg, beaten with a fork. Pulse to combine thoroughly. Remove to a large bowl and with floured hands knead to make sure no lumps remain. Divide the almond paste mixture into 12 even pieces and shape each into a log 3½ inches long.

Preheat the oven to 350°F. Roll out the dough for the crust about ¼ to ½ inch thick and cut twelve 4-by-2-inch pieces. Butter a baking sheet, place these rectangles on it, and top each lengthwise with an almond paste log. Combine dough scraps and roll out ¼ inch thick. With a pie crimper or a knife, cut out twenty-four strips ½ inch wide by about 3 inches long. Using the remaining egg, beaten with a fork, brush along the sides of the rectangles. Place two strips crosswise over each almond paste log, about an inch apart. Gently press the two crusts together with your thumb and carefully brush the strips with egg. Trim the edges of the pastries, if necessary. Bake for 25 minutes, or until golden, turning the baking sheet once during this time. Cool on racks. When cooled, place in an airtight container. These tartlets keep well.

For a modern meal, serve as dessert or as a treat with tea or coffee.

Apple Custard

The consistency of the following custard is reminiscent of tapioca pudding. It has a lovely bright apple flavor.

2¼ pounds Golden Delicious apples

½ cup dry white wine

½ cup water

2 tablespoons salted butter

1 cup coarse fresh bread crumbs without crust, made from a good peasant-style white loaf

5 egg yolks

½ teaspoon ground ginger

2 to 4 tablespoons sugar to taste

Peel the apples, quarter, and core. Cut each quarter into three slices lengthwise and then cut the slices across into small pieces. In a large saucepan, combine the wine, water, butter, and apple pieces. Cook until the apples are very soft. Mash the apples and stir in the bread crumbs, mashing the crumbs as well. Whisk in the egg yolks, ginger, and sugar and cook over low heat, stirring constantly, until the custard thickens, about 3 to 4 minutes. Be careful not to overcook, or the yolks will curdle. Pour into a pretty bowl and serve at room temperature or chilled.

For modern use, serve as dessert with or without some plain cookies, such as the Tea *Cookjes* on pp. 72–73.

Apple *Taert* with Anise in a Cream Crust

Everyone likes the crust, made with heavy cream rather than butter, as much as the filling. Note that the crust recipe must be prepared in two batches.

NOTE: A *taert* is a raised pie nowadays made in a springform pan and between 1¼ and 2 inches high.

For the crust:

4½ cups all-purpose flour

1½ cups sugar

2 egg yolks

2 cups heavy cream

In the work bowl of a food processor fitted with the metal blade, combine *half* the flour and sugar. Run the machine for a few seconds. Stir 1 egg yolk into 1 cup of cream. With the machine running, pour into the flour mixture and process until the dough forms a ball. Wrap in plastic wrap and refrigerate. Make a second batch of dough using the remaining half of the ingredients.

For the filling:

6 Golden Delicious apples, peeled, cut into quarters, cored, and then cut across into slivers (about 6 cups)

½ to ¾ cup sugar, depending on the sweetness of the apples

1 tablespoon ground cinnamon

1 cup currants

1½ teaspoons anise seed, crushed with a rolling pin, or whirled in the food processor

4 tablespoons butter, divided

1 egg beaten with 1 tablespoon water

Preheat the oven to 350°F. Roll out one batch of crust into an 18-inch circle and fit into a buttered 9- to 9½-inch springform pan, allowing the dough to overhang the pan by 1½ inches all around. Place one-third of the apples in the crust. Combine the sugar and cinnamon and sprinkle one third of the mixture over the apples. Cover with one third of the currants, one-quarter of the anise seed (you are going to sprinkle some on the lid), and one-third of the butter, cut into small pats. Make two more layers in the same manner. Roll out two-thirds of the second batch of dough into a 10-inch circle. Place the top crust on the apple mixture, then tuck in the edges to cover the filling completely. Fold in the overhanging edge of the bottom crust and secure it to the top crust all around. Using a paring knife cut out a zigzag pattern all around in the protruding edge. Roll out the reserved dough and cut out a 1½-by-8-inch strip. Cut another zigzag edge on one long side of this piece. Cut out a 2½-inch circle from the middle of the top crust of the pie and insert the strip of dough, curled into a tube, zigzag edge up. It will look like a crown and will form the "chimney" to release steam. Freeze the scraps for later use, or, if you wish, use them to make leaves and flowers to decorate the top crust. Moisten the bottom side of each decoration with a little water before placing on the crust. Brush the entire top with the beaten egg mixture and sprinkle with the remaining anise seed. Place the pie on a baking sheet and bake for 1 hour and 20 minutes, or until the crust is golden and the apples are tender.

For a modern meal, this *taert* is especially good as a filling dessert topped with or accompanied by ice cream or whipped cream. Serve it after a simple meal of soup, or by itself with coffee or tea.

Apricot *Taert*

The original recipe reads: "Take Apricots, peel them and place them in the *Taert* then top with some Cinnamon, Sugar, *Sucade* [Citron] and some Butter and bake a half hour." Apricots are available in supermarkets in May–July and freeze very well. The crust for this *taert,* or sweet raised pie without an upper crust, is deliciously buttery and crunchy and goes well with fruit fillings. Apricots pair beautifully with almond paste; I mixed the paste with cream cheese and used it to cover the crust before the fruit was added. It adds luscious flavor to the *taert.* Citron seems to be only available in supermarkets around holiday time, but can be found online.

> *For the crust:*
>
> 2 cups all-purpose flour
> ½ cup packed light brown sugar
> 11 tablespoons (1 stick plus 3 tablespoons) cold, salted butter, cut into pats
> 2 egg yolks, lightly beaten with a fork
> 1 teaspoon rose water (omit if unavailable)

Lightly butter a 9-inch springform pan. In the work bowl of a food processor fitted with a metal blade, combine flour, sugar, butter, egg yolks, and rose water, if used. Process just until a cohesive dough forms. Press out the dough on the bottom and 1¼ inches up the sides of the prepared pan. Run your thumb around the rim to even it.

For the filling:

3 oz. almond paste (not marzipan)

3 tablespoons sugar

3 oz. cream cheese

1 egg yolk

9–10 apricots, depending on size, peeled, cut in half, pits removed, see below

For topping:

1 tablespoon sugar mixed with 1 teaspoon cinnamon

⅓ cup finely cut citron

1 tablespoon salted butter, cut into small pats

Preheat the oven to 350°F. In a food processor, process almond paste and sugar until finely chopped. Add the cream cheese and egg yolk and process until smooth. Use a rubber spatula to spread this mixture on the bottom of the *taert* shell in one layer. Peel the apricots by dropping them in boiling water for 20–30 seconds and the thin peel will slip off easily. (If you do not want to bother with this extra step, it will affect only the looks of the *taert*, not the taste.) Cut in half and remove the pits and arrange apricots rounded side up in an even layer in the prepared crust. Sprinkle with the sugar-cinnamon mixture and then with the citron. Top with small pats of butter and bake for about 50 minutes or until the crust is golden and the apricots are tender.

For a modern meal: serve with tea or as dessert. Delicious!

Lemon Custard

This is a recipe for lemon lovers.

2 whole eggs

2 egg yolks

½ cup sugar

Juice of 2 lemons, about 4 tablespoons

½ cup plain dry bread crumbs (it is best to make the crumbs by grating stale white bread without crust, because commercial bread crumbs are slightly salty)

2 cups milk

2 tablespoons salted butter, optional

Using an electric mixer set at moderately high speed, beat together the eggs, yolks, and sugar until slightly thickened. Slowly add the lemon juice. Pour the mixture into a saucepan, set over low heat, and bring to a simmer, stirring constantly. Stir in the bread crumbs, then slowly add the milk and butter, if used. Keep stirring and cook the custard for 4 minutes, or until thickened to the consistency of runny porridge. Pour into a pretty bowl and cool.

For a modern meal, serve as dessert with some poached fruit and slices of pound cake, if available.

Peaches in Syrup

The following is a modern recipe that fits in very well with these historical ones.

4 medium-sized peaches

1 cup sugar

1 cup water

Raspberry jam, optional

Peel the peaches. (If you drop them in boiling water for 20 to 30 seconds, the skins will slip off easily.) Cut in half and remove the pits. In a saucepan, combine peaches, sugar, and water. Bring to a boil, then reduce the heat and simmer until the peaches are soft but not mushy. Allow to cool before serving.

For a modern meal, serve two halves and some of the syrup in a small bowl. Drop a spoonful of raspberry jam into each peach hollow. Serve as dessert accompanied by plain cookies or Wafers (p. 75).

Pear *Taert*

Use the same crust as for the Apricot *Taert*. Seckel pears usually appear in supermarkets around November and December.

For the filling:

1 cup currants

12 Seckel pears, or 6 medium pears (about 1½ pounds), ripe but not mushy, peeled, cored, cut into quarters and then into 2 or 3 lengthwise slices (if very large, cut the slices in half crosswise as well)

⅓ to ½ cup sugar, depending on the sweetness of the pears

½ teaspoon dried ground ginger

1 teaspoon ground cinnamon

Place the currants in a small saucepan and cover with water. Boil 1 minute, then remove from the heat and let the currants stand 5 minutes. Preheat the oven to 350°F. Drain the currants thoroughly and combine with the pear slices, sugar, and spices. Spread the filling evenly in the crust. Bake for about 50 to 60 minutes, until the crust is golden and the pears are tender.

For a modern meal, serve as dessert or with coffee or tea.

Plum *Taert*

The filling for this *taert* has a custard-like consistency. The cinnamon and cloves round out the acidity of the plums. Use the same crust as for the Apricot *Taert*.

For the filling:

2½ pounds Italian prune plums, washed

½ cup water

½ to 1 cup sugar, depending on the sweetness of the fruit

3 egg yolks

3 tablespoons salted butter, melted

1 teaspoon ground cinnamon, plus some extra for
sprinkling on top
¼ teaspoon ground cloves

In a saucepan, combine plums, sugar, and water. Bring to a boil, then lower the heat and simmer gently until the plums are very soft. Remove with a slotted spoon, allow to cool somewhat, and take out the pits. Use juice for some other purpose. Preheat the oven to 350°F. Puree the plums in a food processor fitted with the metal blade. Add the yolks, butter, cinnamon, and cloves and process until thoroughly combined. Spoon the puree into the prepared crust and bake for 30 to 40 minutes, or until set. Cool on a rack. Sprinkle lightly with cinnamon before serving.

For a modern meal, serve as a dessert, with a dollop of whipped cream if desired.

Shoemaker's *Taert*

This old recipe that appears in *De Verstandige Kock* can still be found in Dutch cookbooks today.

10 sour apples (such as Granny Smith), peeled, cored, and
cut into chunks
1 cup raisins
5 tablespoons salted butter, melted
¾ cup sugar or to taste
4 egg yolks
4 egg whites, beaten to stiff peaks using an electric mixer
1½ cups plain dry bread crumbs
Sweetened whipped cream, optional

Place the apples in a heavy-bottomed pan large enough to hold them in a layer no more than 4 inches deep. Cover the pan tightly and cook the apples over low heat until they are very soft, *stirring frequently or they will burn.* Using a potato masher, mash the apples and add as much sugar as you think is necessary. Add the raisins and butter, then the egg yolks. Using a rubber spatula, gently but thoroughly fold in the egg whites. Preheat the oven to 350°F. Generously butter a 9-inch spring-form pan and sprinkle with enough bread crumbs to completely coat the bottom and sides. Spoon half the apple mixture into the prepared pan, then sprinkle with half of the remaining bread crumbs. Spoon in the remainder of the apple mixture and sprinkle the rest of the crumbs in an even layer over the top. Bake for about 45 to 60 minutes, or until the cake is firm and light brown. Let cool on a rack before removing the pan sides.

For a modern meal, cut into wedges and serve with or without a dollop of sweetened whipped cream.

Strawberry *Taert*

Note that the crust recipe must be prepared in two batches.

For the crust:
Butter for the springform pan
4 cups all-purpose flour
⅔ cup light brown sugar
22 tablespoons (2¾ sticks) cold, salted butter, cut into pats
4 egg yolks, lightly beaten with a fork
2 teaspoons rose water, if available

Lightly butter a 9- or 9½-inch springform pan. In the work bowl of a food processor fitted with a metal blade, combine *half* of the butter, flour, sugar, egg yolks, and rose water, if used. Process just until a cohesive dough forms. Press the dough on the bottom and 1¼ inches up the sides of the prepared pan. Run your thumb around the rim to even it.

Make a second batch of dough, using the remaining half of the ingredients. Wrap in plastic wrap and refrigerate.

For the filling:
¾ cup sugar
1½ teaspoons ground cinnamon

2 pints of strawberries, washed, hulled, and cut in half
lengthwise

1 egg beaten with 1 tablespoon water

Preheat the oven to 375°F. In a small bowl, combine sugar and cinnamon. Set aside 1 tablespoon for the top. Place the strawberries in a
neat layer in the bottom of the prepared shell. (Pretend you are putting
together a puzzle!) Sprinkle with half of the sugar mixture. Make a
second layer using the rest of the sugar mixture. Between two sheets
of plastic wrap, roll out the second dough portion into a rough 10-inch
circle. Using, if possible, the bottom of another springform pan of the
same size as a template, cut out a neat circle to fit your pan, from dough
about ¼ to ½ inch thick. Reserve the scraps. Peel off the top layer of
wrap and use the bottom layer to help you ease the crust onto the filled
pie, making sure that it covers the rim of the bottom crust all around.
Using a paring knife, gently press the edge of the top crust at ¼-inch
intervals to fuse the top crust to the sides of the pastry. Do not press so
hard as to cut through the crust. Freeze the scraps for later use, or, if
you wish, use them to make leaves and flowers to decorate the top crust.
Moisten the bottom of each with a little water before placing on the
crust. Cut 3 gashes in the crust to let steam escape. Brush the top crust
with egg mixture, then sprinkle with the reserved sugar-cinnamon
mixture. Place on a baking sheet and bake for 30 minutes at 375°F, then
lower the heat to 350°F and bake for about 20 minutes longer, or until
golden. Let cool. The *taert* is best when served the same day it is baked.
It is a bit runny and not quite as neat to serve as a modern-day pie.

For a modern meal, serve as dessert with or without whipped cream
or vanilla ice cream. Supply a spoon as well as a fork.

Miscellaneous, Including Advice on Cooking with Children

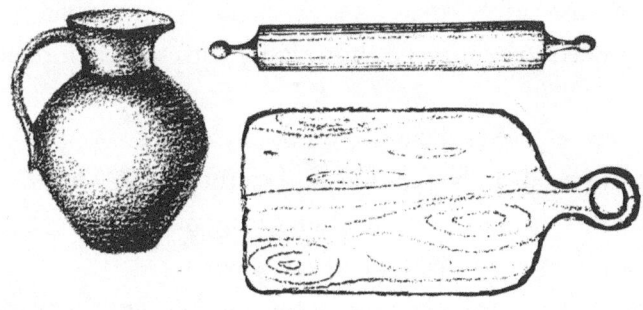

OVER THE YEARS I have found that cooking some of the recipes in the classroom helped in reinforcing lessons on the Dutch colony New Netherland (mandatory in fourth and seventh grades in the State of New York Social Studies curriculum). For fourth grade the curriculum says for students to "investigate colonial life under the Dutch." Here some of the cookie recipes might come into play. For seventh grade, students will examine "social characteristics" and are "to compare and contrast with other cultures." A good example for this might be the recipe for pumpkin cornmeal pancakes: the Dutch used the Native American corn in a way they were used to and mixed the cornmeal (as if it were wheat, barley, or rye) with milk and made the batter into pancakes.

Some of the recipes in this book I especially recommend for cooking with children are: Coleslaw, Fried Green Leaves, Pumpkin Cornmeal

Pancakes, Three-in-the-Pan, Letter Cookies, Caraway Cookies, Currant Cookies, *Koecxkens* (Fritters), *Krakelingen* (Pretzels), and Tea *Cookjes*.

Advice for Cooking with Children

Throughout the text, I have indicated recipes that are suitable to cook with children. Cooking with children is not only fun, but there are other good reasons: cooking helps with hand-eye coordination and finger-thumb dexterity; it reinforces academic skills; it teaches nutritional and cultural concepts; it cultivates responsibility and independence; but above all it leaves a feeling of pride and accomplishment.

Before beginning your cooking project, explain and follow some simple health and safety rules:

• Hands need to be washed thoroughly with soap before beginning to cook.

• Hair needs to be tied back and out of the way.

• Clothing needs to be secured so it cannot catch fire.

• Potholders need to be used when lifting pots.

• Pot handles need to be turned sideways.

• Knives need to be picked up by the handles, not the blades.

• Stove needs to be turned off as soon as cooking is finished.

Recipes for fruit confections, nut candy, and sweet spiced wine are included in this section, as well as instructions on how to prepare homemade mustard.

Candied Quince Squares

Candied quince is a delicious confection that will keep all winter long in a cool, dark, and dry place.

> 4 quinces, well scrubbed
> Sugar

Place the quinces in a large saucepan and cover with water. Boil gently for about 25 minutes, or until the fruit is tender and the skins start to burst. Remove to a rack, cover with paper towels, and cool to lukewarm.

Cut into quarters and remove the cores and any hard parts. Scrape the pulp into a bowl, discarding the skins, and mash thoroughly. Weigh the pulp and mix with an equal weight of sugar. Place in a heavy saucepan and bring to a full boil. Boil, stirring constantly, until the mixture stiffens and shifts as a mass when the pot is tilted, about 15 minutes. Be careful not to overcook the quince; if you do, it will have a tacky texture and a caramel flavor. Sprinkle a baking sheet thickly with sugar. Spread the hot quince mixture on the sugar in an even layer about ⅜ inch thick. When the mixture is cool enough to handle cut it into neat 1-inch squares. Sprinkle another baking sheet with sugar and place the squares upside down on the sugar. Heat the oven to 175°F. Sprinkle the squares lightly with sugar and place in the warm oven for 20 minutes. Turn the oven off, wait 20 minutes, then turn the oven on again for 20 minutes longer. Repeat this process until the squares are no longer soft and sticky, turning them periodically and sprinkling them lightly with sugar if they seem very moist. (If this method seems too cumbersome, leave the squares in the oven overnight with the oven light on. Check in the morning; if not dry, turn the squares over onto another baking sheet sprinkled with sugar and place back in the oven with the light on; repeat until dry.) When the squares are done (dry), again sprinkle them lightly with sugar and place them between sheets of wax paper in an airtight container and store in a cool place. They will keep for months, providing they were dry.

For a modern meal, serve the squares after dinner as you would bonbons.

Candied Young Walnuts

This recipe originally appeared in "De Verstandige Confituur-maker" (The Sensible Confectioner), an appendix to *De Verstandige Kock*.

Dutch culinary historian Marleen van der Molen Willebrands used it to develop the following recipe.

> 2 pounds unripe walnuts (see below)
> Cinnamon sticks
> Whole cloves
> Sugar

Pick large unripe walnuts before June 24, as indicated in the original recipe (June 24 is the name day of John the Baptist), before the woody shell is formed. (The shell should be soft enough to prick with a long needle.) For the next step, wear gloves to prevent your hands from turning brown. Peel off the green shell until you reach the white kernel. Using a needle, puncture the nuts in several places. Place the nuts in a large bowl or pail and cover with water. Allow to stand for 9 or 10 days, changing the water several times a day. This soaking takes out the bitterness. Boil the nuts in ample water for about 10 minutes, or until soft. Drain and spread them on a rack to dry. Stick a thin piece of cinnamon stick and 2 cloves in each nut. (To make thin pieces of cinnamon stick, use a knife to split the sticks lengthwise and then break each into 1½-inch pieces.)

Prepare enough sugar syrup to cover the nuts, using two parts sugar to one part water. Bring to a boil and boil the nuts in the syrup for 5 minutes. Remove them from the heat and let them stand in the syrup for 24 hours. Place the nuts in sterilized jars. Reduce the syrup until thick and pour it, while boiling hot, over the nuts until they are completely covered. Close the jars while hot, and process according to the manufacturer's instructions. Place them in a cool, dark spot. Be patient; they will be at their best by Christmas time.

For a modern meal, serve them after dinner as you would bonbons, or as a treat anytime.

Cherry Fruit Leather

This recipe originally also appeared in "De Verstandige Confituurmaker" (The Sensible Confectioner). It has the title "To Preserve the fruit-marrow of Cherries, Plums, Apricots, etc. for a whole year." The recipe below follows its instructions except for using modern aluminum foil instead of the "glazed tiles" called for in the original. The fruit leather can also be dried in a 175°F oven or as indicated for the Quince Squares. Clearly, it can be made with all kinds of fruit.

   1½ pounds cherries, stems removed

Place the cherries in a large saucepan, set over low heat, and stir frequently until they release their juices. Simmer until "the outer skin comes off and the meat has become a thick porridge," about 30 to 40 minutes. Rub them through a sieve, and discard the skin and pits. Pour the puree on oiled baking sheets in a very thin layer and place in the sun. When dry and only slightly sticky, cut into 1-inch strips. Carefully pry up one end with a thin knife, then gently pull each strip up and away from the baking sheet. Place on a piece of wax paper or oiled aluminum foil and roll up with the paper or foil. Store in an airtight container.

For modern use, give the leather as a special treat to all good children, young or old!

Kandeel

This traditional celebratory drink for the time a baby is born, is still part of Dutch culinary tradition. *Kandeel* was served by the royal family when the present Crown Prince (now King) Willem Alexander of the Netherlands was born in 1967. Recipes for this festive drink appear under the Anglicized name of *"condale"* in several of the manuscript cookbooks that were handed down in families of the descendants of the first Dutch settlers of New Netherland. Here is my adaptation.

> 1½ cups water
> 10 whole cloves
> ¼ teaspoon ground mace
> ¼ teaspoon freshly grated nutmeg
> Two 3-inch cinnamon sticks
> Zest of 1 lemon, removed with a vegetable peeler
> 6 egg yolks
> ½ cup sugar
> 1 bottle (750 ml) Rhine wine

In a small saucepan, combine water, cloves, mace, nutmeg, cinnamon, and lemon zest. Cover and simmer for 1 hour. Strain through a fine sieve and set aside. Heat water in the bottom half of a double boiler. In the top of the double boiler, beat the egg yolks and sugar until foamy. Place the pan with the egg mixture on top of the pan of boiling water, making sure that the bottom of the top pan does not touch the boiling water. Whisk in the spiced liquid and continue to beat until the mixture thickens. Slowly beat in the bottle of Rhine wine. Serve hot. If the drink separates upon standing, stir with a spoon or a tall cinnamon stick.

For a modern meal, serve this festive drink at the end of the meal with "sweetmeats," such as the candied quince squares (pp. 88–89), or use the recipe on the happy occasion of a baby's birth.

Mustard

Here is a modern recipe for an old favorite.

> 2 tablespoons yellow mustard seed
> 2 tablespoons black mustard seed
> 2 tablespoons white wine vinegar
> 2 tablespoons honey
> 1 tablespoon water
> ½ teaspoon freshly ground black pepper
> ¼ teaspoon salt, or more to taste

Combine all ingredients in a blender and grind with a pulsing action. The mustard should be coarse and retain some whole seeds. Remove to a small container and refrigerate. It will thicken after standing.

For a modern meal, it is an excellent accompaniment to ham, pork, or sausage.

Raspberry Brandy

The following drink recipe appears in several of the manuscript cookbooks of descendants and calls for large quantities of raspberries and brandy. Here is a scaled-down version. The drink is very good after about a week, but continues to improve with age.

> Three 10-ounce packages frozen raspberries, or 2 pounds fresh raspberries, cleaned

1 fifth brandy

2 cups sugar

Rinse a large screw-top jar and lid with boiling water. Combine all ingredients in the jar. Place the jar on your kitchen counter and shake it every time you pass until the sugar has dissolved. This will take about 24 hours. Allow to stand for another day or so. Then rub the mixture through a sieve, lined with a large paper coffee filter, to remove the seeds, pressing down to extract every bit of juice. You might have to use several filters before the liquid is clear. Rinse the jar with boiling water again and pour the fruit brandy into it. Allow to stand for another 7 days or so. It improves with age.

For a modern meal, serve this intensely fruity drink after dinner. It is especially nice when paired with a creamy custard with whipped cream and some cookies. Dark chocolates or bonbons also combine well with the strong raspberry flavor.

Spiced Wine or *Hippocras*

Hippocras, a sweetened spiced wine, is a drink with a long history. Recipes for it appear in both Dutch and English cookbooks and mentions of it being served at elaborate banquets go back to the Middle Ages. It can be made with both red and white dry wine. The recipe that follows, created by culinary historian Stephen Schmidt, is based on one by Robert May in *The Accomplished Cook* of 1660/1685.

8 3-inch cinnamon sticks

4 large or 6 small nutmegs

4 teaspoons whole cloves

7 whole peppercorns

2 quarts of pleasant, neutral-tasting wine (such as Pinot Grigio, but not Chardonnay, which is too oaky)

⅓ cup chopped peeled ginger

1½ teaspoons dried rosemary

4 cups sugar

Combine cinnamon sticks, nutmegs, cloves, and peppercorns in a sturdy plastic bag ("freezer bag") and whack with a small heavy skillet or hammer until coarsely crushed. Pour the wine in a large jar and stir in the crushed spices, then add the ginger and rosemary. Cover and let steep for 24 hours (but no longer). Strain through a fine-mesh sieve, shaking the spice debris in order to salvage as much wine as possible. Pour 1 cup wine through a paper coffee filter. Change the filter, then pour through another cup of wine. Repeat until all the wine is filtered. Mix the wine with 4 cups sugar and let stand until the sugar completely dissolves, which will take several hours.

The wine will keep indefinitely in the refrigerator. Yield: about 2½ quarts.

Spiced Wine or *Hippocras* (hot)

Here is my hot version of the drink; it is not quite as heavily spiced as the recipe above, but makes a comforting drink for a cold evening.

> 2 bottles Merlot or another red wine to your liking; white wine may be used as well
> 1 whole nutmeg
> 2 cinnamon sticks, each about 3 inches long
> 1 tablespoon coriander seed
> 2 slices ginger, each about the size of a quarter
> 2 tablespoons honey
> ½ cup packed dark brown sugar

Pour half a bottle of the wine into a nonreactive saucepan. Put the dry spices in a heavy-gauge plastic bag and crush coarsely (I used a hammer for the nutmeg). Empty the bag into the wine and add the ginger, honey, and sugar. Bring to a boil, then remove from the heat and allow to stand for 24 hours. Pour through a fine sieve into a saucepan, add the remaining wine, and heat through.

Traditionally served with wafers for dessert, *hippocras* is best offered nowadays as a hot drink on a cold winter's evening when everyone is gathered by the fire.

References
❖❖❖
Indexes

References

Battus, Carolus. 1593. *Eenen Seer Schonen/ende Excellenten Cockboeck.* 2d ed. Dordrecht.

B. G. 1763. *Volmaakte Onderrigtinge, ten dienst der Koek-Bakkers of hunne Leerlingen.* Wed J. van Egmont Op de Reguliers Bree-Straat.

Blankaart, Stephanus, M.D. 1633. *De Borgerlyke Tafel Om lang gesond sonder ziekten te leven.* Amsterdam, n.p.

Burema, Lambertus. 1953. *De Voeding in Nederland van de Middeleeuwen to de Twintigste Eeuw.* Assen: Van Gorcum.

De Cierlijcke Voorsnijdinge Aller Tafel Gerechten. 1664. Amsterdam: Hieronymus Sweerts.

De Verstandige Kock. 1683. In *Het Vermakelijck Landtleven.* Amsterdam: Marcus Doornick.

Elting, Anna Maria. May 8, 1819. Manuscript cookbook. Archives, Historic Huguenot Street, New Paltz, New York.

Hasbrouck, Hylah. 1840. "Hylah Hasbrouck's Receipts" (manuscript cookbook). Archives, Young-Morse Historic Site, Poughkeepsie, New York.

Kalm, Peter. 1966. *Travels in North America: The English Version of 1770.* Edited by Adolph B. Benson. 2 vols. New York: Dover.

Lefferts, Maria Lott. n.d. "Mrs. Lefferts' Book" (manuscript cookbook). Archives, Brooklyn Historical Society, Brooklyn, New York.

Manuscript Cookbooks Survey, Project of the Pine Needles Foundation of New York, accessed Aug. 16, 2019, https://www.manuscriptcookbooks survey.org/.

Morse, Elizabeth Ann Breese. 1805. "Mrs. E.A. Morse, Her Book April 10, 1805" (manuscript cookbook). Archives, Young-Morse Historic Site, Poughkeepsie, New York.

Peyster, Anna de. n.d. Manuscript cookbook. Archives, Historic Hudson Valley, Tarrytown, New York.

Riley, Gillian. 1994. *The Dutch Table*. Rohnert Park, CA: Pomegranate Artbooks.

Rose, Peter G. 1993. *Foods of the Hudson*. Woodstock: Overlook Press.

———. 1998. *The Sensible Cook: Dutch Foodways in the Old and the New World*. 1989. Reprint, Syracuse: Syracuse Univ. Press.

———. 2009. *Childhood Pleasures: Dutch Children in the Seventeenth Century*. Syracuse: Syracuse Univ. Press.

Schoonmaker, Jemima. n.d. Manuscript cookbook. Archives, Historic Huguenot Street, New Paltz, New York.

Tannahill, Reay. 1973. *Food in History*. New York: Stein and Day.

Van Cortlandt, Anne Stevenson. n.d. Manuscript cookbook. Archives, Historic Hudson Valley, Tarrytown, New York.

Van der Donck, Adriaen. [1655] 1968. *A Description of the New Netherlands*. Edited with an Introduction by Thomas F. O'Donnell. Syracuse: Syracuse Univ. Press.

Van der Groen, Jan; Nijland, P.; and Anonymous. 1683. *Het Vermakelijck Landtleven*. Amsterdam: Gijsbert de Groot.

Van Rensselaer, Maria Sanders. n.d. Manuscript cookbook. Archives, Historic Cherry Hill, Albany, New York.

Van Sterbeeck, Franciscus. [1668] 2006. *Traktaat van de Kampernoeljes, genaamd Duivelsbrood*. Edited by Marleen Willebrands and Anno van 't Hoog. Hilversum: Uitgeverij Verloren.

Van Winter, Johanna Maria. 1971. *Van Soeter Cokene*. Haarlem: Fibula Van Dishoeck.

Vorselman, Gheeraert. [1560] 1971. *Eenen Nyeuwen Coock Boeck*. Annotated edition. Edited by Elly Cockx-Indestege. Wiesbaden: Guido Pressler.

Wheaton, Barbara Ketcham. 1983. *Savoring the Past*. Philadelphia: Univ. of Pennsylvania Press.

Index for Essay

Index for Recipes

Foreign words are in italics and recipe titles are capitalized.

105

Culinary historian **Peter G. Rose** was born in the Netherlands and came to the United States in the mid-1960s. She has worked as a food writer; she contributed a syndicated column on family food and cooking to the New York–based Gannett newspapers for more than twenty years and has written articles for magazines such as *Gourmet, Saveur,* and the *Hudson Valley Magazine.* She is the author of several books on the subject of the Dutch influence on the American kitchen, including *The Sensible Cook: Dutch Foodways in the Old and the New World* and *Matters of Taste: Food and Drink in Seventeenth-Century Dutch Art and Life.* This is her tenth book.

She is the recipient of the 2002 Alice P. Kenney Award for research and writing on the food customs and diet of the Dutch settlers in New Netherland. She lectures nationally and internationally on a variety of topics related to Dutch and Dutch-American culinary history, including at the Smithsonian Institute, the National Gallery, the Peabody Essex Museum, Houston Museum of Fine Arts, Bryn Mawr College, New York University, and the Culinary Institute of America, and in the Netherlands, at the University of Amsterdam and the Mauritshuis Royal Picture Gallery in The Hague, among others.